USING MANAGEMENT GAMES

USING MANAGEMENT GAMES

Second edition

Chris Elgood

Gower

Published by
Gower Publishing Limited
Gower House
Croft Road
Aldershot
Hampshire
GU11 3HR
England

Gower Publishing
Old Post Road
Brookfield
Vermont 05036
USA

CIP catalogue records for this book are available from the British Library.

Typeset in 10pt Century Old Style by Poole Typesetting (Wessex) Ltd., Bournemouth and Printed in Great Britain by The University Press, Cambridge.

Contents

Preface

This book presents in paperback form the text that appeared as the first half of the fifth edition of *Handbook of Management Games*. That publication was a hardback, containing also a reference section giving brief descriptions of almost three hundred available games. It included indexes that enabled readers to track down material relevant to their needs. The two-part construction of the Handbook, though logical and helpful for some readers, meant that those who wanted only a discussion of the subject also had to purchase material in which they had no immediate interest. It is for such readers – those who want to know what management games are, and what types can be found, and in what ways they can be useful – that this general text has been separated out to become USING MANAGEMENT GAMES.

Readers should be careful to avoid making choices about which sections to study just by following up a familiar title. This warning is offered because the field to which the book gives the description 'Management Game' is one afflicted with a low level of agreement about terminology. Controversy is frequent, and what one person calls a management game may be referred to by another as a simulation, or an exercise, or a structure, experience or just an activity. Helpful ideas can be overlooked if one has rigid expectations about what the terms mean, and uses those expectations to judge sections as relevant or irrelevant. A significant excursion into the text is usually worthwhile.

As in *Handbook of Management Games*, the pronoun 'he' is used to mean 'he/she' throughout.

Chris Elgood

Using Management Games

1 Types, traditions and terminology

APPARENT DIVERSITY

There is no simple answer to the question 'What is a management game?' They are all attempts to represent – in an environment away from the immediate pressures of work – selected aspects of the management task. Since management is a complex and varied activity, the aspects selected also differ. And since there are many different ways of representing reality, the format of games likewise varies. If you were to demand 'Show me a management game being played' you would probably find yourself observing small groups, but those small groups might be doing any of the following:

- Debating and writing lists
  This is a typical activity in ranking exercises. Players have to decide the relative importance of certain items: each individual makes a list, and then the players try to reach a group solution.
- Debating and putting cards into piles
  In card-sort exercises, players classify items rather than rank them, and put like with like.
- Problem-solving
  This involves working as a group to complete an imposed task. The tasks vary and many have a tangible element. It is less likely that the players will remain in constant discussion-group format. Different parts of the group may be in different places, doing different things.
- Building something
  Some exercises simulate a construction activity by using model materials. Groups can be found building towers, bridges, etc. out of Lego bricks.
- Manufacturing (e.g. making paper aircraft)
  There are exercises which require the establishment of a small production line, which is judged by its ability to turn out real objects. Like building exercises, these involve movement, perhaps requiring absences from the work area while enquiries are made or materials found.
- Sitting at a board with dice and tokens

Board-based decision-making games use dice, cards, tokens and symbols.

- Sitting at a microcomputer
  Computer-controlled games give details of an imaginary company and call for keyboard-entered decisions about how it should be run.
- Debating policy and completing forms
  The traditional business management exercise requires decisions about the running of an imaginary company. These can be many and complicated and need careful thought. The decisions are written on a form and passed to a controller. Players are likely to be sitting amongst a mass of paper, poring over complex sets of figures.
- Acting
  Some games require players to act out roles created for them such as employer/trade unionist, salesman/customer or recruiter/applicant. This will look like a rehearsal for a play.
- Making face-to-face deals
  Trading games require constant movement between customer and supplier and competitor. The likely appearance is near-chaos, with people running from room to room waving 'orders' or carrying simulated 'deliveries'.
- Running through the woods with paint guns
  Outdoor management development takes many forms. As well as the traditional rock climbing and sailing, there are more game-like activities which offer a sanitized version of gang warfare.

COMMON INTENTIONS

Behind the variety of games there is quite a high level of common agreement about what is being attempted and why it is thought likely to work. The publicity materials of game suppliers yield an interesting mix of ideas.

> 'Exercises and games ... allow theory to be put into practice in a 'risk free' environment.' (Gower)
>
> 'Business games ... provide an extremely powerful learning experience combined with a high degree of excitement and enjoyment.' (J.H. Handley, ICL-Cranfield Business Games Ltd)
>
> 'Simulators ... create work simulations, so that trainees can safely learn from accelerated experience.' (Peter Dye Associates)
>
> 'Gaming simulations ... increase role awareness and the importance of interpersonal relationships and communication.' (Mott MacDonald)
>
> 'Realistic business simulations provide memorable challenges and allow trainees to transfer the skills and experience learnt back to their businesses.' (April Training Executive)

> 'The participants gain insight into their own behaviour as they interact with others and develop sensitivity to the perceptions, needs, goals, management styles – in short the behaviour – of others'. (Training House)

> 'Games . . . have built-in learning potential about the subject matter itself or about the managerial and cooperative process.' (Chris Elgood)

> '[Management Games] . . . are designed to do three things . . . illustrate . . . demonstrate . . . and make a significant improvement in communication between and within the groups of people taking part.' (Edit 515 Ltd)

> 'People learn more when they are enjoying themselves. It's not just true of children. It's true of executives, managers – of everyone.' (Management Games Ltd)

The richness of the field is partly due to the fact that it is influenced by several different traditions.

DIFFERENTIATION BY TRADITION

Management games reveal a scientific tradition and a social science tradition, but predating them both is a pragmatic tradition of experiment and practice. More recently, ideas have been drawn from an entertainment tradition. A common result is that anyone who arrives in the field of 'management games' thinks that their route towards it was somehow the 'natural' one.

A problem associated with this convergence is that practitioners rooted in one tradition are not always aware of their own attitudes and assumptions. They may view the work of other traditions as 'wrong' and overlook cooperative opportunities from which they might otherwise gain.

THE PRAGMATIC TRADITION

The construction of practice situations to fill the gap between receiving instruction and attempting a task appears to be instinctive. It is clearly visible in the make-believe games of children, and we claim to see it in the play of young animals. It is not a product of modern science, and the earliest hunter/gatherers probably had some sort of practice routine whereby they tried to improve their chances of making a kill. We use simulation quite naturally as a response to situations in which we will have to display skill and take risks. In order to gain the value of practice and experience without those risks we construct something which is recognizably 'like' the reality while differing from it in consequences. A historical example is the quintain, the training exercise of tilting used by medieval knights which required them to gallop towards a post and strike with their lance a sandbag that was extended from the post on a bar. The bar was fixed so as to revolve on top of the post, swinging the sandbag round. A successful strike and controlled follow-through allowed the knight to thunder past unharmed: a wayward strike and clumsy follow-through produced a retaliatory strike from the sandbag.

Such 'practice runs' vary as widely as the human activities they are meant to assist, because the original objective of their design is to produce something *like* each specific reality. Accordingly, there is no commonality in appearance. Nor is there any theoretical definition or standard to which they must conform. There are just two conditions they must meet – usefulness and an acceptable cost.

Usefulness and cost, which are both pragmatic considerations, have a refining effect on simulations. People ask analytical questions like 'What are the key skills that this device is meant to foster?' Less important objectives are thus discarded, with the features that supported them, and cost decreases. Expensive features are scrutinized to see whether something else will do instead, and some aspects are merely represented rather than directly imitated. Reality is pushed a little further into the background and the simulation becomes more like a game. We cheerfully use the title 'war game' to describe a simulation which is nothing like real war. It is played in a classroom with maps and symbols, because what is being modelled is not 'war' in a total sense but the analytical and decision-making process essential for senior officers. By contrast, there are battle simulations which require private soldiers to crawl close to the ground while real bullets are fired over their heads. The key factors are need, purpose and cost: the general needs to practise strategy – the private needs an unforgettable lesson in keeping his head down. Each activity retains the features that are deemed important, while keeping the costs of doing so acceptable to an adequate level of reality. In flight training, for example, the consequences of poor training are very serious, and realistic simulators are built at great expense. Thus the pragmatic approach can extend from quite crude scenarios to highly scientific simulations and it is not really possible to say that any one approach is in itself 'better' than another. The correct question is 'What are we trying to achieve?' or to put it another way, perfect modelling is *not* the objective of the pragmatic tradition. This is better stated as 'To help people do better tomorrow than they did yesterday'.

Games with this pragmatic base are found mixed up with other products that are in a sense more reputable because they are rooted in a recognized body of knowledge. Creators of this sort of game are sometimes critical of those with a more pragmatic approach because they are not the result of serious study and argue that until something has been properly researched the 'best' way of handling it is not known. Therefore the fact that something 'works', and improves a situation, may mean that it is concealing something that would work better still, and it is turning people away from further search, and therefore doing harm rather than good.

THE SCIENTIFIC TRADITION

The scientific tradition is derived from scientific study and has its roots in operations research. The desire is to find theoretically optimum solutions that will improve on 'seat of the pants' pragmatism: a commonly cited example is the development of the convoy system to protect ships at sea against enemy action. Operations Research simulates reality by expressing it in terms of mathematical relationships. It aims and sometimes succeeds (as in the convoy case) at finding a method which is better in practice than the experience-based alternatives. The tradition was influential in universities and business schools (aided by the emergence of the computer) and a specific type of management game emerged, which sought to create situations in which the best-known practice (which was carefully researched) would obtain the best results. Some of these devices were set up to allow competition between different teams. All of their strategies were taken into account, so that they affected each other and affected the environment. The competitive element made it natural to speak of them as 'games'. However, there is still a valid distinction between business simulations and business games. The former do not involve interaction between the decisions of different teams and it is 'the real environment' which determines the relative success of a player's decisions. Using this approach it is theoretically possible to research the market and build a set of rules which will judge in the same way as would the market. Where interaction is allowed, opposing teams may behave in a manner that *would not* happen in real life, but they still have an effect on the results of other teams. They distort reality, and prevent those other teams from experiencing a wholly realistic response.

The human element did not feature strongly in early management games of the scientific tradition. Few current users of such games would argue that to grasp the theoretically 'right' answer to a business problem is enough, but the knowledge tag has stuck because it is broadly true. Games derived from this tradition do emphasize hard knowledge. Their creators might argue, if attacked, 'However skilled you may become at managing people, and winning cooperation from others, you won't succeed as a manager if you don't *know* certain facts and have certain intellectual skills.'

Games of this sort are often about concepts and abstractions: one cannot touch or handle a price/demand relationship or a lead time. Instead they use the standard conventions by which human beings make pictures, or representations of reality: words and numbers to signify quality and quantity and mathematical rules to simulate cause/effect relationships.

THE SOCIAL SCIENCE TRADITION

Games in the social science tradition reflect the development of social science in the second part of this century, and are concerned with what happens between people and between groups in emotional rather than intellectual terms. An influential force was the T-group, a training method which demonstrated to those taking part that our actions are not always governed by logic but are partly a response to inner, psychological needs.

Two characteristics of this field of study contrast sharply with those of the scientific tradition. First, we can 'see' human behaviour in a much more immediate way than we can ever 'see' a market relationship. And perhaps because of this, we do not have a means to 'represent' human behaviour in the way that we have developed for abstractions. Crudely, in knowledge based games we use representational methods because we *do* have them and because we *do not* have reality: in behavioural games we *do* have reality to work with and we *do not* have adequate representation techniques. Therefore it is not surprising that games about behaviour have a quite different outward appearance. They sometimes involve data, briefing papers and physical objects, but these items only exist to set boundaries within which the players will act. It is the actions and attitudes of the players that are the subject of study, not the item about which they are interacting. It is the **process** of human interaction which is significant, not the **content** (subject matter) about which it takes place.

Games about behaviour tend to demand less time than games about knowledge, and often have a narrower, more precise aim. Some, for example, seek to help players discover aspects of themselves and their behaviour that are not particularly welcome. Thus they gain from drama, and from a quick feedback cycle.

THE ENTERTAINMENT TRADITION

Games and simulations have always benefited from the fact that they are fun to play, but in education and training this was seen as a characteristic needing control. If students enjoyed games too much, it was felt their attention might be distracted from the serious business of learning. Today, more credence is given to the idea that enjoyment of an activity creates a positive attitude towards the activity itself *and the learning that accompanies it.* To illustrate the idea in a school setting, if maths lessons are found to be enjoyable (for whatever reason) then the concept of 'maths' acquires a good image, more effort is put in, better results are achieved, and more maths is learned. Practitioners who want to create this upward spiral ask openly and aggressively 'What do people enjoy? What gives them their kicks?' An obvious place to look for models is in entertainment, including sport. Some management games now look remarkably like popular television shows, and one firm marketing management games makes an explicit claim to be employing 'the notion that people enjoy competitive games' as a management tool (LMG International).

DIFFERENTIATION BY USAGE

Most games can be used in different ways and for more than one purpose. In fact it is fair to say that the method of use is a greater variable than any inherent quality of the game itself. This is because much of the learning comes from reflecting afterwards on the experience, and the nature of that experience is influenced by the choices made by the facilitator. Therefore the skill of such a person is doubly important. Facilitators can alter the experience, and alter the value people receive from it by their handling of post-event reviews. Three purposes are common.

PROMOTING KNOWLEDGE AND SKILL

Reasons commonly given under this heading are to reinforce instruction, to integrate functional viewpoints and to improve decision-making.

Reinforce instruction

Games and simulations about running an imaginary business are used to help players discover whether they have grasped, and are able to apply, what they have learnt theoretically. With this purpose can be grouped the concept of allowing students to discover for themselves new lessons that perhaps they have not been told in class. With it, too, goes the concept of practice: trying out those skills that are hard to grasp in theory but become more obvious when applied to a specific case.

Help players see the broad picture

This is similar to the first objective, but it needs to be distinguished because it is the most common declared purpose for using the 'imaginary business' type of game. Most business education is based on a functional/departmental split and many managers rise in an organization through a single specialized channel. Development practitioners therefore find a widespread need for a device that will 'Show them how it all fits together'.

To improve decision-making

The information presented to the players of a management game is often structured to create a 'time window' between making decisions and discovering the result. This makes it possible to review the decision clinically *before* the results are known. It is advantageous, because outcomes do not always prove that a decision was 'good' or 'bad'. Both in real life and in games they may be affected by chance, or by unforeseeable factors, so that a theoretically good decision produces a poor result (or the reverse). When that happens, the analysis of the decision is apt to be too strongly coloured by the outcome, and proper deductions are not made. The game format can avoid this.

INCREASING BEHAVIOURAL SKILL

It is human to be concerned with oneself and one's own objectives, and to pay inadequate attention to the effect one's behaviour is having on those who observe it. The social sciences have had a large influence on management training by demonstrating some critical facts. Facts such as these:

- Many of us do not realize how we appear to others.
- Many of us adopt behaviours to achieve short term goals that are counterproductive in terms of other goals because they damage relationships.
- Many of us do not realize that working together demands a range of skills that are not intellectual in nature but, rather, social: skills in building relationships

and in creating an environment where people feel comfortable, valued and secure.

Many exercises are centred upon single skill items, of which the best example is perhaps 'listening skill'. This means the intellectually simple but behaviourally difficult task of maintaining and displaying a state of sympathetic attention until one fully understands another person's point of view. Other exercises concentrate, for instance, on the human tendency to make assumptions and treat them as facts, or the tendency to evaluate ideas by reference to the status of the person offering them rather than their inherent merit.

Where behavioural skills are being studied under a general title like 'cooperative skills' or 'teamworking', longer exercises may be used, and even the shorter type of knowledge-oriented business game. The situation may therefore arise where a particular device might be used by one practitioner for one purpose and by another person for a different purpose.

GIVING PLEASURE AND PROMOTING TEAMWORK

The words 'giving pleasure' have been used deliberately here because a lesson only now becoming accepted is that *good teamwork and pleasure are closely related.* While motivation and teamwork have been discussed separately it has been inadequately emphasized that motivation as a general phenomenon is all about rewards – and teamwork can provide them. These are not so much the traditional material rewards, but the psychological rewards that make people feel 'I like working here' and give them good feelings about Monday morning rather than fear and misery.

Enjoyment was gradually seen to have an intrinsic motivational value. The brief to a game designer acquired a different emphasis. Where the request had previously been 'I want an exercise that will teach them XYZ' one began to hear phrases like 'I don't demand that you teach them anything special. I just want them to have an enjoyable time, working closely together on something that is broadly work-related.' This was essentially a request about teambuilding, recognizing that people work better together (especially in terms of communicating) if there is knowledge and respect between them *as human beings rather than just as office-holders.*

Once the idea of 'getting to know each other' was seen as reasonable, the use of exercises not based upon work gained status. For work is the area in which people already know most about each other: what they *do not* know – and what may increase their mutual liking and respect – lies outside work. Thus activities were developed in which the objective was to provide opportunity – opportunity for people to display existing skills and acquire new ones, to help each other, to cooperate, to attempt new challenges and to participate in group success. The feeling that one is a valued, and necessary member of a team, and a contributor and a friend is psychologically rewarding. Circumstances can develop in which team membership provides these rewards – and is *expected* to provide them *irrespective of the task the team is attempt-*

ing. The situation has become the motivator, not the task objective or an extrinsic reward. So one of the factors determining the value of an activity is whether team members gain psychological rewards from it or, crudely, whether they have fun.

This underlines one aspect of the current debate about the improvement or amendment of the traditional bureaucratic organization. The way in which bureaucracy has come to confine and limit human opportunity is seen as intolerable and inefficient. There is a need to enrich known forms of association so that people are allowed to contribute as fully as they are able.

TERMINOLOGY

The different traditions each have their own terminology, and specific connotations are attached to it. Definitions therefore remain a significant problem, and users of management games sometimes appear to be talking at cross purposes. In an attempt to minimize the confusion, words have been used in this book with the following connotations:

1. *Device* is used to cover every activity that might conceivably be designated 'game'.
2. *Activity* is used as a synonym for device, but employed when the game described is less complex – less worthy of the 'structured' and 'engineered' feeling that goes with 'device'.
3. *Simulation* is used to describe activities in which any of the following characteristics seem to dominate:

   - A physical means of reproducing, off-the-job, the phenomenon being studied.
   - A precise focus on a single, specialized phenomenon, so that the lessons are not obviously transferable to other areas.
   - Absence of direct human opponents, the challenge being 'player versus environment' rather than 'player versus player'.

   Simulation is also used as a default term when a device cannot be given a more precise and readily comprehensible label. The term is sometimes augmented by describing the method of representation by which simulation is achieved. Thus 'Simulation – paper and pencil' is distinct from 'Simulation – physical structure'.
4. *Game* is used to describe activities in which some or all of these characteristics are prominent:

   - Human, or humanly controlled, opponents, whose actions have an effect upon each other and upon the environment.
   - An emphasis on competitiveness and 'winning'.
   - An emphasis on pleasure, humour and enjoyment.

- A repetitive cycle of making decisions and encountering a result, allowing the hope of improvement and of 'doing better next time'.

5. *Business game (or simulation)* is used for any such device having an industrial, commercial or financial background.
6. *Management game (or simulation)* is used for such devices when they are concerned with the planning, management and control of any organization or project in circumstances where profit is not the dominant measure of success.
7. *Exercise* is used for devices covering specific and well-defined subject areas, specially when these are one-off experiences with no repetitive cycle.

Management games vary almost as much as 'games' in the ordinary everyday sense, but they share a broad objective: they are all intended to help people learn about management and organization and to promote skills that will increase organizational efficiency. Well used, they justify the time they require.

2 Games and human behaviour

RECOGNIZING THE INFLUENCE OF PERSONAL BEHAVIOUR

There are some devices which enable people to grasp basic truths about human behaviour in general, or about themselves as individuals. These emerged as a reaction against the mechanistic view that people in organizations behave in a rational, logical way at all times. That is, the assumption that once a person has contracted to do a job he performs the tasks for which he is paid, irrespective of emotional feelings. If working life becomes too uncomfortable he leaves, but while he is there he controls his feelings and acts 'normally'. This view suggests a lack of interest in how one's behaviour is perceived by others. If it is 'correct' in terms of accepted procedures, that is sufficient.

Ideas changed, and a desire grew to show that this mechanistic view was fallacious and that our feelings affect our behaviour (and impact upon others) in all sorts of way. One line of approach was to gather a group together and remove *all* the excuses that people typically invoke to deny the influence of personality and emotion. If that was done, then whatever happened in the group had to be the consequence of personal behaviour and emotional interaction. So a training group made up of diverse people might find itself with no task to attempt and no leader to give instructions. There was no **content** to discuss, so **process** (what went on between group members) became the focus of attention. It worked, in the sense that it demonstrated the universal presence and influence of personal feelings.

The next step was to introduce a minimum level of content, and show how the emotional undercurrents produced by personal behaviour affect group achievement. The group was given a task to complete, but it was carefully designed to exclude 'contaminating' factors. The idea of contamination is best illustrated by considering a group that has one expert on a subject about which nobody else knows anything. As long as the task given is related to that subject, power and influence will remain with that one person. The others may feel inadequate, ignored and resentful, but admitting such feelings is very difficult because they seem unreasonable. 'After all', goes the mental argument, 'If this man really is an expert then the sensible thing is to let him carry on with the job and not waste his time with ignorant questions and self-concern.

We are here to get the job done.' Desire to avoid such contamination produced exercises that were abstract in nature (allowing no scope for specialist knowledge) or even destroyed the would-be expert by invoking a different rationale.

GAMES THAT SHOW US OUR FAILINGS

The actions that make other group members unhappy are often linked to the self-oriented nature of human beings: the tendency to assume that our own way of seeing a subject is automatically the right way, the obvious way, or the only way. The concept of 'making assumptions' therefore features prominently in exercises that reveal to us our failings, as in the following examples.

AN INFORMATION-SHARING EXERCISE

A group of people are given details about the candidates short-listed for a job. All of them have the same list, but each one also has a short text that is personal. These are about the same length, have most of the lines in common, and may well be handed out stapled to the candidate list so that everybody, it seems, is in an identical position. In fact, each personal brief contains a special item of information and when *all* the data available to the group has been integrated it becomes obvious that only one candidate is really suitable. Some common occurrences in this exercise are as follows:

- Assumption of a dominant role by somebody who has experience of selection work, or committee work.
- Introduction of personal values by various group members who say 'I believe a candidate must have this quality' – without there being any reference to it in the text.
- Disregard of anybody providing information that conflicts with the currently accepted line of argument.
- Disregard of information coming from anybody who is temporarily of low status in the group.

When the right answer is reached (or revealed by the facilitator) the message received by participants is often that they unconsciously made wrong assumptions about the nature of the exercise. They thought it was about expert judgement when it was really about cooperative behaviour, and because of this incorrect assumption they tackled the task in an ineffective way.

The effect of a wrong assumption can be shown by comparing alternative behaviours towards low status members. Persons believing the exercise to depend on expert judgement, and seeing themselves as such an expert, might behave in a superior way to such a member, allowing that member little opportunity to speak and taking little notice when he does. This would not be likely to encourage a positive contribution. A person seeing the exercise as one demanding participation from everybody would be much more considerate, probably taking great care to 'bring in' low status members and evaluate their ideas seriously.

Many exercises feature the need for people to share information, but this type takes 'information sharing' as its title because the need for sharing is deliberately contrived in order to create what is sometimes called a 'structured experience'. The group is, as it were, 'seeded' by giving different items of data to different people so that they have 'private' information. The most common means of achieving this is through different written data for each person, but more elaborate approaches exist. People can be directed to different data sources, or information can be presented in different ways, such as one person having information in writing and another having complementary information in the form of a logic diagram, so that the connection is not immediately obvious.

A PROBLEM-SOLVING EXERCISE

Another device for revealing and reflecting our habits consists of five squares of cardboard, each cut into three geometric shapes. They are mixed up and put into five envelopes. Five group members are then sat round a table and told that their task is to pass shapes between them until each member has a composite shape in front of him and all those composite shapes are identical. They have not seen the original squares. Rules are usually imposed to prevent talking or obvious sign language. The only officially allowed action is for one person to offer a piece of cardboard to another. The design is such that there is no alternative solution. Three reactions that may be observed are as follows:

- People being very concerned with their own success or lack of it – looking at colleagues only in order to pick up clues that may help solve their own problem.
- One or more people who believe they have 'solved the puzzle' sitting complacently behind their shape to watch the others struggling. (It is possible for an individual square to be made up in such a way that it is impossible to construct the other squares.)
- One or more people who are convinced of the 'right' answer and show extreme irritation because another group member apparently cannot see an option that they believe to be obvious.

The exercise demonstrates our comparative weakness in cooperative skills, particularly when we have been led to regard part of the job as being 'ours' in an individual sense.

Problem-solving exercises like this have no single source and vary from mental challenges aimed at individuals to elaborate investigations that require a team approach. The simpler exercises are effectively in the public domain and most easily found in 'collections' such as the volumes of 'Activities' published by Gower and the 'COMPENDIUM' of Management Games Limited. A few exist individually in 'packaged' form where suppliers have built a structure round them or when users may be expected to value the convenience of prepared materials. An additional source of these and of more complex games is the journal of SAGSET, *Simulation/games for learning.*

THE PRISONER'S DILEMMA

A generic title for a type of exercise that examines cooperation and competition is 'The Prisoner's Dilemma'. One version requires that small teams should be 'paired' with each other and asked to choose between strategies 'A' and 'B'. There is a game fiction surrounding the event which states that if both choose A then both teams score 0 points; if both choose B then each scores 2 points; if one team chooses A and the other chooses B then the scores are 4 and 0 respectively. There is a negotiating stage in which representatives from each pair meet and discuss what they will do. Having studied the conditions, each will be aware of the chance of the double-cross: that is, agreeing to choose A, choosing B instead, and hoping that the other party has not done the same. Since there is no point in declaring an evil intent, the negotiating session normally ends with both agreeing to choose B, and to score 2 points each. The representatives return to their teams and consider what they will actually do. Their choices are written down and passed to the facilitator, who then reveals the scores. The process is repeated, perhaps with the stakes being doubled each time. The exercise obviously strains the trustfulness of each team, and there is a powerful urge to strike immediately – the argument being 'If we double-cross them successfully now, then we may all score zero points for the rest of the exercise, but at least *they* won't get ahead of *us*.' Learning points that emerge are likely to include the following:

- The human tendency to identify with close and familiar groups, perceiving any such group as US and all other groups as THEM.
- The self-centredness of individuals and groups. It is quite common for the groups to make an automatic assumption that their own objective (and the objective of the other group) is to maximize *group* points and never even discuss the possible objective of maximizing *pair* points.
- The difficulty of building trust without knowledge or obvious common interest.
- The difficulty of committing oneself to a policy that can be totally frustrated by somebody else.
- The problems that arise when any division of responsibilities has to be made within a group that is nominally pursuing a single goal.

This activity looks to the observer like neither of the two previous exercises. There are small groups debating earnestly – without any written material – and messengers flitting between them. The activity is very much in the public domain and critical discussions about it can be found in the literature.

GENERAL TEACHING OR PERSONAL LEARNING?

There are subtle differences in the objectives with which a facilitator might use exercises such as those discussed. They can demonstrate forms of human behaviour that most of us exhibit and thereby offer lessons of general application. They also permit a focus on the individual behaviour of group members, and make it possible to highlight the transactions that take place between them. The lessons are concerned with what one person said and did at a particular moment, and what effect it had upon others, how they perceived it, how they interpreted it, how they felt, and so on.

The user needs to avoid confusion between these objectives, for one of them (demonstration) is allied with a traditional and didactic approach to learning while the other relies upon reflective learning taking place in the mind of each group member. Both approaches involve opportunities and risks. The idea of an exercise as a demonstration is perfectly valid, but one has to remember that there is no certainty of it developing in the desired way. Once the activity has been set up, the sequence of events is determined by the players and intervention by the facilitator is not helpful. Thus the user who thinks 'This will teach them that . . .' may end up like the chemistry teacher who tells the class the litmus paper is going to turn blue – and then it doesn't. He may be seeking to make some vital point, and then finds that the exercise has provided no 'ammunition' with which to support it. The best strategy is to become so well acquainted with the exercise that one understands the range of likely events, is able to use what *does* happen constructively, and so widen the scope of discussion to include some of the outcomes that did not occur. The diagram shown in Figure 2.1 shows the need for the game user to be aware of a wide range of possible player reactions and to avoid concentrating on one only.

The other purpose of the exercises – to concentrate attention upon the direct interpersonal transactions between group members – is easier in one way and harder in another. There is no need to worry about the exercise proceeding in a particular direction and 'proving' a particular point. The purpose is to study interpersonal behaviour, and there will be plenty of that, whatever course the exercise follows. But

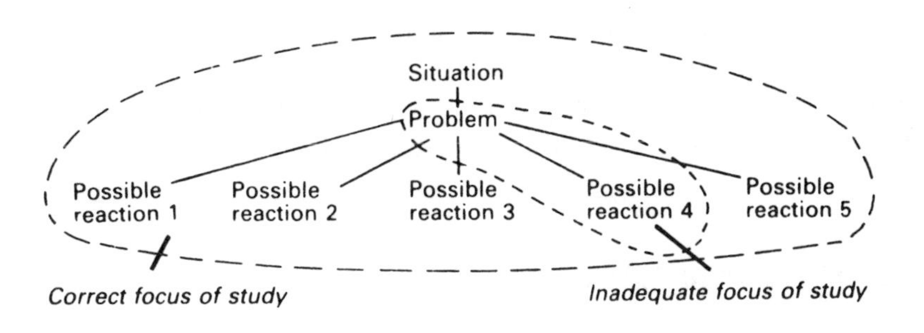

Figure 2.1 **Forms of human behaviour in a particular situation**

what about learning from it? The greatest strength of this experiential learning is that it sometimes enables people to recognize facets of their own behaviour, and its effect on others, that they would not otherwise grasp. That is, it is personal learning – different and distinct for each individual – and not general theoretical learning. It is also quite often unwelcome, because the characteristics we do not know about ourselves are mainly those about which nobody has told us, and the reason they have not told us may be that we have shown clear signs of not wanting to be told. Acceptance of lessons of this sort takes time, needs a constructive attitude, and reflection about what has happened. It cannot be handled by an instructor saying 'This is what you must learn from the experience.' Why?

- The instructor may very well be wrong. Not being conversant with the private thoughts of the parties to an interaction, the instructor cannot know why something was said, how it was received, or what were the attitudes of the parties. He can only offer his interpretation of what he saw and heard, which is no more likely to be right than anyone else's.
- Interpretations of behaviour are always deniable. Since nobody except the person involved knows exactly why something was said or done, it is always possible to adduce some reason quite different from that which has been imputed.
- Criticism that is both unwelcome and deniable can be counter-productive, making the person concerned more determined than before to reject the changes that have been urged upon him.

Little has changed since Robert Burns lamented our inability to see ourselves as others see us. We still construct for ourselves a pleasing self-image: we still resent and reject incoming information that damages it. We are not too keen on questions such as:

- Did you realize you were behaving that way?
- Did you realize what effect your behaviour was having on your colleagues?
- Do you sometimes behave like that in real life?
- Do you feel you want to make any changes to the way you conduct yourself?

The task of the facilitator is to create a climate in which incoming information can be accepted, and can become the subject of constructive reflection by each individual. This concentration on the individual means that there is no common message, nothing the game user can use to substantiate a general statement like 'This is what you must learn.' Results depend very much upon the attitudes and learning skills of participants.

IDEAS FOR THE FACILITATOR

Over the years, expertise has been built up which assists in the creation of a constructive attitude and the furtherance of reflective learning.

CLEAR INTENTIONS

It is absolutely necessary to distinguish between the two objectives of demonstrating phenomena and creating an experience for reflection. Where the objective is to demonstrate, the facilitator ought to be able to say why he intends to use an exercise and what sort of benefit he hopes students will gain. The worst that can happen is that he will have to confess to wrong judgement or lack of skill. This is not as bad as having to admit that the thinking was not undertaken in the first place.

Where the objective is to encourage personal, reflective learning the facilitator should studiously avoid any authoritative posturing and look for a questioning, non-judgemental role in which participants find it natural to speak freely.

A COMMON LANGUAGE

Open and constructive comment about the behaviour shown in an exercise is easier if participants have a common language in which to discuss it. One way of providing this is through a behaviour typing discipline, so that people know the meaning of 'proposing', 'supporting', 'blocking', 'gatekeeping' and so on. Another way is through personality questionnaires that make people aware of their own characteristics and 'legitimize' the way they behave. A useful device of this sort is the strength deployment inventory of Elias Porter, which categorizes behaviour in a simple and understandable way and presents all the categories in a positive light. Any form of behaviour can then escape condemnation as 'wrong' and be seen instead as an 'overused' strength. This helps to reduce defensiveness.

There must certainly be a common understanding about the single word 'perception'. People have to be aware that everything we see and hear is immediately modified by our own mental standpoint and that we do not make decisions on evidence – only on the basis of our perceptions. This understanding makes a significant difference to the discussion of behaviour, because it enables one person to comment upon another without making accusations. Statements made within the context of this agreement always admit the possibility that the 'receiver' of a signal may be misjudging the 'sender'.

HONESTY

A significant facilitator error is to make exaggerated statements about an exercise. These are easily seen through and create an over-critical, unconstructive attitude. The truth about all these exercises is that they offer no guarantee. People use them because they are well worth the risk, but the risk element is never wholly absent, and from time to time every facilitator will experience what feels at the time like failure. Perhaps the exercise will develop in a way that has little behavioural interest, or perhaps he will be unable to frame questions that are both sensitive and revealing. However, people like to have some indication of what an event is concerned with, and one form of introduction which is generally helpful is to refer to one's own exercise experience. The form of words might be like this:

> 'This is an exercise from which people have in the past learnt valuable lessons in the area of XYZ. I can't tell you in advance what is going to happen this time, or in what way it is going to help anybody in this group. But my experience leads me to believe that if you take it seriously, and then examine what happened, you will gain something worthwhile from it.'

Related to the issue of honesty is the fact that some of these exercises contain an element of deception: the participants are being placed in a situation where the dice are loaded against them. In some cases a trick is being played on them (in the information-sharing exercise described, the concealment of the fact that there are separate briefs), and in most of them they are being watched by somebody who knows beforehand what they are likely to do – somebody in a superior knowledge state who can easily be credited with a patronizing attitude. It is not an enjoyable situation and only justifiable by the gains that participants will, it is hoped, make. It can be helpful to acknowledge and excuse this element of deception.

EXPOSING ONESELF

Sometimes in such exercises people are put in a position where they don't know what will happen and fear that they may expose aspects of their character that they would rather keep hidden. One way the facilitator can help is to take the lead in talking about his feelings and exposing his weaknesses. Others then feel less badly about joining in.

GROUND RULES FOR REPORTING

Describing the behaviour of others, that is giving feedback, can be accomplished crudely or with sensitivity. There are two ground rules of special usefulness:

1. The person giving feedback should strive to make objective, factual statements about what happened and not allow them to be coloured by his interpretation.
2. The person giving feedback should always explain the effect behaviour had upon him rather than impute motives to the other party. It frees the person being discussed from the implication that he intended an effect and reduces the risk of resentment.

LETTING OTHERS DO THE WORK

Despite the low-key title of 'facilitator', a person in this role is seen by students, and usually sees himself, as in a position of authority. It is natural to feel that this requires one to make a lot of telling points – in fact to talk rather much and to be able to answer questions. However, if the facilitator can just keep quiet a little bit longer it is amazing what students will do for themselves. Whatever opinion is expressed, or question asked, there will be somebody in the group who has a useful comment to make. This is true even when some member is being excessively critical and saying, in effect, 'This is a load of rubbish'. There is sure to be somebody else who thinks the reverse, and will say so if he is given some time. And since the exercise is presented on the basis that people are to extract learning for themselves, the facilitator can afford to throw responsibility back at the group. It is quite in order to make comments like 'I'm not supposed to be doing all the work. Let's hear what others think!'

USE OF OBSERVERS AND ANALYTICAL INSTRUMENTS

It is usually valuable to use non-participating observers to report and discuss what they have seen. They can be given a written brief to direct their attention, or they can use one of the behaviour-typing disciplines to add precision to their observation. Management Learning Resources Ltd offers a group process document in their Group Process Questionnaire game to be used after such exercises as a means to put some order and discipline into the reporting. A useful general purpose observer's questionnaire is shown in Figure 2.2.

AVOIDING DIDACTIC STANCES

One of the most damaging facilitator errors is to make categorical statements about other than observable facts. Whatever people say and do in such exercises, their reasons come from within and are unknown to anybody else. Observers interpret what is said and done, and can speak about those interpretations, but they cannot *know* and are on dangerous ground if they pretend to. The facilitator must avoid discussions that are approaching 'You did', 'I didn't.' A few disengaging phrases are needed like 'Well, only you can tell us, and we must accept what you say'.

ABILTY TO DRAW REAL-LIFE PARALLELS

So far as these exercises illustrate common forms of human behaviour, it follows that those forms appear in organizational life. It is usually possible to show how some of the imperfections demonstrated in the exercises would reveal themselves in the organization. For instance, the failure to pick up and make use of ideas offered by low status members is a common organizational fault. So is lack of interest in the problems of

1 Did the group maintain high standards of work or was it easily satisfied?

1 2 3 4 5 6 7

2 To what extent did group members really listen to each other?

1 2 3 4 5 6 7

3 Did attempts to influence the group come mainly from one, or a few people (score towards the LH end of the scale) or did they come from all quarters (score towards the RH end of the scale)?

1 2 3 4 5 6 7

4 Was I able to contribute to the group without having to fight for noise space?

1 2 3 4 5 6 7

5 Was disagreement within the group more often expressed and resolved (score towards the RH end of the scale) or was the tendency to sweep it quietly under the carpet (score towards the LH end of the scale)?

1 2 3 4 5 6 7

6 To what extent was work with this group enjoyable?

1 2 3 4 5 6 7

7 To what extent did you feel it was proper to express your feelings in this group?

1 2 3 4 5 6 7

8 To what extent did the group members exhibit concern for the group as an entity rather than concern for themselves as individuals?

1 2 3 4 5 6 7

9 Did you feel that the group was working as a team and trusted one another?

1 2 3 4 5 6 7

Figure 2.2 A typical questionnaire

other departments. So is communication failure, like not reaching a common understanding about the meaning of a policy or objective.

Further comment on possible objectives and attitudes of tutors and facilitators is offered in Chapter 10.

3 Games to promote knowledge

The previous chapter referred to games designed with a limited knowledge content in order to facilitate the study of behaviour. This chapter examines a number of simpler game formats, primarily in respect of their use to promote subject knowledge.

The traditional way to promote subject knowledge is by direct instruction – the lecture. It allows much knowledge to be broadcast to a sizeable audience, the hope being that the listeners will then know more about the subject and be better able to handle it in practice. Compared with the lecture, games suffer from two serious disadvantages:

1. They require a longer time allocation to cover the same amount of material, and;
2. They are less rigidly programmed than a lecture, so there is no guarantee that all the points a lecturer might wish to make will emerge clearly or be given sufficient emphasis. They cannot be 'nailed down' in the way a lecturer might write 'bullet points' on a blackboard.

Those who use games for promoting subject knowledge would put forward contrary arguments such as the following:

- Games can have considerable subject knowledge actually built into them. They can pose a problem, demand an answer, and respond to the answer with a judgement that is knowledge-based and 'right'. Thus the experience can substitute for the lecture and serve as an object lesson. The student learns by experience rather than by hearsay. There is also plenty of opportunity for the facilitator to emphasize learning points as the game progresses, and in a formal review session.
- There is a massive difference in student motivation. All that can be guaranteed from a lecture is that knowledge will be transmitted. There is no guarantee that it will be listened to and understood. By contrast, participants in a game are actively involved: they are interested, and they are themselves operating on the subject matter. Even if less is being officially 'transmitted', much more is being 'received'. Motivation is further enhanced by the expectation of enjoyment and freedom of action that is associated with the word 'game' – and the team concept that eliminates the fear of isolation.

- Games are usually a group activity and thus there is discussion between the participants. This means that the views of many people are being considered, rather than just the views of one person. The ideas put forward by group members may lack knowledge and authority, but that does not make them valueless, because the process of understanding demands that one forms links between what one already knows and what one is being offered. That process may receive more help from discussion with somebody operating at one's own level than it can from an expert: the gap can be bridged from the learners' side as well as the tutor's.
- Game enthusiasts would argue that perhaps there is less authority in what is learnt by games than when it is propounded directly by some knowledgeable speaker, but that this is outweighed by increases in the breadth of learning and the deeper internalization that comes from active participation.

It will be apparent that the arguments in favour of games rest very heavily on beliefs about student motivation. Game devotees assume that players will become interested and committed, thus assuring a high quality of discussion and making it unnecessary to 'hammer home' the learning points.

Central to the alleged connection between interest, activity and learning is the concept of experimenting, achieving a result, and – by analysis – discovering. One standpoint from which to examine different types of game is the extent to which they demand, and respond to decision-making. (The game titles used here will appear again later on, examined from a different angle.)

THE DECISION-MAKING CONTENT OF CERTAIN GAME TYPES

DISCUSSION GAMES

Players receive a description of a real or imaginary problem and must decide what should be done about it. It may be a problem with a clear-cut answer ('Was this person discriminated against?') or it may allow several credible solutions and the exercise of judgement. An authoritative comment follows the players' answer, based on known facts, expert opinion, or on a consensus developed from extensive use of the game. It is not always precise, but it allows players to feel 'We did that well', or 'We missed that one.'

IN-TRAY EXERCISES

Participants receive an assortment of problems – in writing – representing the contents of the 'IN' basket on an office-holder's desk one morning. The task is to decide what one will do about each item, record the chosen action and state the order in which one made decisions. It can be undertaken individually, or by small groups. The method adds a dimension to the discussion exercise because of the need to assess priorities. For instance, it is not enough to take the right action on one matter if, by attending to it, some other time-critical item is neglected. It is very clear with the in-tray exercise that decisions are being made. The origin of the judgements made is much the same as for discussion exercises – informed opinion.

This reliance on opinion makes the traditional form of the in-tray exercise a little weak: many decisions are being made and none of the responses are actually generated by the game rules themselves, as opposed to external judgement. The microcomputer, and the concept of electronic mail have altered those circumstances. It would now be possible to create a computer-based in-tray in which there are predetermined consequences for whatever action is taken on an item, at whatever moment in time it occurs.

DATA BANK EXERCISES

These are based on describing a problem and providing only part of the relevant data. Items are held back by the administrator and made available only in response to a specific request. They demonstrate the danger of tackling problems too rapidly, and with inadequate information, when more could be discovered by thoughtful investigation. They call for a recommendation, or decision about the problem as in discussion games, but are enriched by the fact that participants do or do not conceive the possibility of obtaining extra data and do or do not achieve it by formulating a precise question.

RANKING EXERCISES

Players are asked to set a list of resources, ideas, people, or activities in rank order from the most important to the least important. The usual quantity is ten. The best-known ranking exercise is Desert Survival, requiring the notional survivors of a plane crash to rank ten salvaged items in order of importance for their survival. There is an expert answer, and comparing it with the order chosen by the players allows a quantified measure of success, if desired.

CARD-SORT EXERCISES

Players receive a pack of cards, each identifying one item from a homogeneous set of qualities, people, artefacts, or circumstances and are instructed to sort these into given classifications. The Melrose-Northgate exercise Profile consists of 75 cards containing statements about a manager. The task is to choose the thirty most important statements and type them as 'personal' or 'organizational' or 'interpersonal'. There is a suggested answer with which player choices can be compared.

PROGRAMMED SIMULATIONS

A problem situation is described and some possible courses of action. Players must choose between the allowed options and then receive predetermined comment on what they have done. Programmed simulations develop the problem through several stages, but treat each stage as a separate incident: even if a playing team makes a 'wrong' decision it still encounters the next stage in exactly the same manner as do competing teams. Scoring involves counting up the incorrect choices, perhaps weighting the system to penalize those that are seriously wrong rather than just imperfect.

MAZES

Maze games use the limited option format of programmed simulations, but a choice leads to a new state as well as to comment upon the choice made. In the maze, playing teams are effectively told 'Because you decided to do *that*, *this* situation has now arisen. What are you going to do about it?' If the original choice allowed five options, then there have to be five second-stage scenarios. If those all have five options, then there have to be twenty-five at the next stage, so a maze could become extremely complex and difficult to handle. In fact the problem is reduced by feedback loops and some degree of duplication in the options. Scoring is achieved by counting the moves taken to reach a successful outcome, or accepting failure. One of the early mazes was the Joe Bailey Action Maze, featuring Joe's poor attendance record. Success was identifying the cause of Joe's problem and cooperating with him in an attempt to improve. Failure was Joe's response 'I quit.'

HOW TO 'MAKE A GAME OF IT'

The main points so far offered in support of games are that learning can be 'discovered' as well as 'received' and that the participative form allows greater learning through discussion with peers. There is also an alleged benefit from the keenness and application deriving from a desire to win. If these arguments are wholly or partly accepted then it is necessary to ask 'How can it be done? How can the game environment be invoked?'

One has to look to games as a model, and identify those features that are powerful motivators and will also transfer readily to the management training world. Some progress can be made just by techniques of association, but a deeper approach is deliberately to import known enjoyable features.

ASSOCIATIVE LINKS

The main associative link is language. Just the use of game-like words has an effect – as in the exercise Par Excellence. This is a discussion exercise based on eighteen work-related problems to which students must provide an answer and on which they can be scored. The questions are not about golf, but just talking about the golf concept of the par score, the outward nine and the inward nine creates pleasing images (at least to the golfer) and makes the exercise seem less like a schoolroom test.

Other games use the format of a playing board in very much the same way. A throw of the dice allows a player to move a token across squares, and some of the squares are marked with instructions like 'Production Problem'. The player whose token lands on such a square asks the administrator for a Production Problem Card and has to provide an answer to whatever problem it poses. The interaction between administrator and player is little different from that in a test at school, but the associations are more pleasant.

IMPORTATION OF ENJOYABLE FEATURES

Management games have developed pragmatically, and the fact that they incorporate a range of enjoyable features seems to be a result of natural selection rather than conscious planning. Some users may never have asked the questions 'What do people enjoy? What gives them their kicks?' The list of enjoyable factors given below is partly experience-based, and partly borrowed from motivational theory. In some cases there is comment intended to forge links with management games of the types already mentioned, and these links are matters of detail rather than of 'course design' at a macro-level. This is not an accident, and the detail matters. The motivation of learners is an on-going variable that can cause them to feel more interest or less interest on an instant basis *as an event is progressing*. The fact that some pleasant feature has a short-term motivational effect is *not* unimportant: it may maintain interest in the event at some moment when it would otherwise be lost, some significant development missed, and the participant lose touch thereafter with what was going on. Participants need reinforcement of their commitment at regular intervals, and this can be drawn from encountering relatively transient experiences as they work through the activity. A phenomenon that is not assessed at a conscious and intellectual level is not thereby made unimportant.

Freedom

People prefer to exercise personal choice, contrasting such freedom most strongly with direct control by another person. In this sense even submission to the chance throws of a board game offers more freedom than exists in a classroom. The player may not be in control, but nor is he at the mercy of a human authority. At least the dice are impartial.

Optimum challenge

This is a phrase from the literature of motivation, meaning that people enjoy those challenges that are appropriate to their ability: not challenges at which they are certain to fail, not challenges that are too easy, but the sort of challenge that makes a person feel 'On a good day I might just succeed at this'. Some games allow the players to choose the type or complexity of a question and, in a sense, decide what level of risk they are prepared to take in pursuit of what level of reward.

Activity and influence

People like making things happen – influencing the world around them and seeing things happen because of what they have done. A term from motivation theory is 'effectance motivation'. In a management game the opportunity may be very minor – moving a token on a board, conducting a simple negotiation, or making some challenging statement. But the comparison being made is with the totally static environment of direct instruction in which the learner has no opportunity to act or to influence outcomes. Just taking up a token, and looking around to one's colleagues and saying 'Are we all agreed then?' makes one for an instant the focal person.

A decision point

People like the challenge of having to commit themselves, of reaching some moment at which they must act irrevocably, and be judged by the result. Decisions are central to management games: they have been mentioned before and will be mentioned again.

Feedback

People like to receive rapid, attributable and actionable information about the consequence of their decisions. This is another direct link to motivation theory, which holds that people like to see the outcome of their actions. It is noticeable that games which offer instant feedback are very popular. One reason might be that people who receive instant answers tend to be powerful people. Another might be that there is a closer mental connection between the reasons that prompted a decision and the game judgement upon it.

Competition

Provided there is some hope of emerging creditably, people enjoy the challenge of competition. In one sense this is identical with the idea of optimum challenge (above) but there is also an element connected with social interaction. After a competitive game it is not only the winners who enjoy the dialogue. Every superior comment from a winning team is matched with cheerful allegations of cheating or undeserved luck from the losers. And both can feel enriched by the competitive experience because it has made them perform better than they would have otherwise done.

Opportunity to succeed

People like the opportunity to learn from experience and to make repetitive attempts until success is achieved. Once that success comes, the frustrations experienced in reaching it are largely forgotten. Game users are sometimes in doubt about whether or not to help a team that is doing badly. Giving help, in such circumstances, seems to be the better option, usually triggering a feeling of pleasure expressed in terms like 'We know how to do it, now!'

Uncertainty/excitement

People enjoy encountering chance. A large number of popular games and sports include elements of chance as well as skill. It creates hope – the hope of sometimes winning when reliance on skill alone would mean a boring and demotivating succession of defeats

The suggestion is that in many cases the attractiveness of a management game lies in the fact that it offers the players these elements of enjoyment. The point of presenting the argument is twofold:

1. It offers a serious reason for apparently 'non-serious' features. It provides an answer to those who would reduce the fun element in games on the grounds that they do not contribute to the serious business of management learning. It shows that they do contribute, but that they impact on knowledge-gain indirectly, through their effect on motivation.
2. Given acceptance of the argument, it allows more knowledgeable and deliberate game design. It enables one to ask and answer the question 'What can we do to make this activity more fun?'

GAINING KNOWLEDGE – HAVING FUN

As an example, consider how the popular game Trivial Pursuit takes what might in other circumstances be a deadly boring general knowledge test and makes it into a game that people play voluntarily, for fun, and in which they learn from each other and from an 'authority'. First, it can be a team game, allowing the pleasure of working with a small group of friends and assigning specialist roles within that team. Next, it has a colourful board and tokens to move around on it. There is a chance element, because of the die throw, but the player can choose in which direction to apply the die throw and there are choices about what type of question to attempt. Further, there is a collecting element – successful answers win tokens that build into a full set, and the competitive position of the teams is obvious to all. The game is relatively long, so one can always hope to improve, and each question stands on its own so that one is not penalized because of past errors.

LESSONS FROM THE MEDIA

Though it is not always possible to apply them, there are valuable lessons to be learnt from the media. Highly popular TV shows take material that might come straight out of school or college textbooks and create shows that have high viewing ratings, with participants scrambling to get on the stage. They are able to do this because their brief (with which they start the game creation process) is a brief to entertain. This position, and the unique resources that they can draw upon, enable them to provide enjoyment factors additional to those previously listed. One can deduce from TV shows that some people, at least, find the following attractive:

- Prominence
  Being, for however short a time, the focal person – the one at whom everybody is looking.
- Association
  Being in the company of famous people.
- Rapid action, feedback and drama
  Short questions, quickly answered and results shown dramatically on a scoreboard.
- Speed, skill and risk
  Having to commit oneself rapidly (finger on the button) without ponderous reflection.
- Interaction
  A question 'passing' from one side to the other, or the option to take/not take a question.
- Sensory excitement
  The aesthetic pleasure of lights, colour and music.

The world of the TV game show is different from the world of the boardroom. It is less different from the atmosphere of the company conference, when people are assembled at an off-the-site location, much money is being spent and the objective is at least in part to enable people to enjoy themselves as a token of appreciation of hard work. In such circumstances organizations can and do borrow tricks and techniques from the media.

GAMES MECHANISMS TO FOLLOW

Some of the features mentioned above refer to the circumstances created by game-playing rather than to the mechanisms by which games are made to work. Is there anything in these mechanisms that is intrinsically motivating? If so, it may enable one to use management games better, to modify them or even create them. There are five particular strengths that well-proven games – those that have lasted for decades or even centuries – possess:

- They create a decision-making situation quickly and easily, often by means of well-understood conventions.
- They contain within themselves everything that is necessary for making the decision and determining the consequence.
- They use irrevocable decisions, and signal the making of decisions very clearly.
- Each decision has an impact upon the state of the game, making the post-decision state different from the pre-decision state. The decisions are therefore dynamic.

- They allow the possibility of scoring, winning and losing, through the operation of an impartial mechanism, voluntarily accepted.

The extent to which management games successfully borrow these characteristics influences the way in which players respond to them. Some connections can be made with the types of management game mentioned earlier.

THE DECISION-MAKING SITUATION

For decision-making to be interesting, it has to be better than guesswork but still involve an element of doubt. Knowledge must be available, but there must be scope for effort and skill in recognizing that knowledge, from which a benefit must be won.

Card games allow everybody to know the nature of the information (the suits and the identities within the suits) but prevent players from knowing the location of the cards not in their own hand. Card games have rules, and these enable players to observe each other's actions, deduce from the actions what cards those others are likely to have, and prepare their own strategies accordingly. Because there are known boundaries to the exercise (the suits) it becomes possible to have comparatively simple rules that still allow sophisticated playing choices. It is easy to enter the game environment.

Board games make a great deal of information openly available to all players through board layout, cards and tokens. By the use of dice an element of uncertainty is introduced, so while everybody can see the present state it requires foresight, and the estimation of probabilities, to play well. As in card games, entry is quick and painless because of well-understood conventions.

Word games use an instantly available body of common knowledge. Everybody can play, but there is great scope for playing better or worse.

Users and creators of management games should be concerned about the question 'How are players provided with the right mix of information and opportunity?' If the process is a long-winded one, requiring a great deal of study and research, motivation is likely to be low. If the process is elegant and economic, motivation will be higher.

The most obvious case of transfer is the use in management games of the playing board format – adopted with little modification. But card-sort exercises and ranking exercises are also of interest because they exploit instantly familiar concepts (putting a finite number of items into categories, or into order). Every device that allows a player to feel quickly 'I know what I am supposed to do' is good. The alternative – confusion and uncertainty – is bad.

BEING SELF-CONTAINED

Knowledge that all eventualities are provided for in the rules contributes heavily to the game-like image. It relates to the concept of freedom, in that players have full responsibility for their fate. They may well not be in control of it, being unable to judge all the options correctly, but at least they feel that the facts are in front of them and they are not going to be arbitrarily upset by an extra-game influence. This is the difference between game formats that assess decisions by the judgement of the administrator and formats in which player decisions generate a response through known rules.

The critical factor is not subjectivity, for rules are themselves subjective in that they represent the judgement of a writer. It is the two concepts of constancy (the rules are not going to change) and disclosure (the necessary decision-making data has been made available). This is why discussion games are a little weak: there is always the feeling that in the review session the administrator may produce additional data which makes people feel 'Oh well, if I had only known *that* I would have made quite a different recommendation.' The same factor works to a degree in data bank exercises, for it is often left to the administrator to decide whether a player has been sufficiently specific in a request.

THE SIGNALLING OF DECISIONS

Both card games and board games have marked moments of decision. A card is played, or turned up. A die is thrown and a token moved, or money paid over. There is a physical indication that something has been done. Everybody is watching what happens, everybody knows what has been done, and it is irrevocable. Game users and designers should ask themselves 'Is the decision-making mechanism clear and obvious or uncertain and ambiguous?' The former is much better for player motivation.

Of the management games described, programmed simulations and mazes are the strongest in this respect because there is the least possible variation in the choices, and the distinction between the chosen and the not chosen is clearest. In a ranking exercise, it is possible to have the expert's 'number 1' as the playing group's 'number 2' and make light of the error by saying 'That's not bad at all. We might have put it at number 10.' And in card-sort exercises the feature is weaker still because the large number of cards makes it very unlikely that one will get the answer totally 'right' and the drama of the event is reduced.

DYNAMIC DECISIONS

Each decision modifies the state of the game, moving it onwards and creating a different situation from that which previously existed. This is particularly evident in card games, where the playing of a single card – adding just one item of information to what players know already – can force dramatic reassessments of policy. Game users and designers should ask themselves whether a device has or can have this characteristic.

Of the management games described in this chapter only the maze is game-like in this way. The others are single stage exercises, or multi-stage exercises in which there is no inter-stage modification.

WINNING AND LOSING

The critical qualities of a scoring mechanism are that it should be understood, accepted, and impartial. A person who takes part under these conditions is in fact demonstrating his freedom to make decisions and his courage to endure the outcome. This, in its way, is a motivating experience.

The difference between winning and losing is most dramatic when there are only two options, and the issue has maximum seriousness, for example living or dying. This is perhaps why some users of survival exercises like to set a level of agreement with the expert answer that acts as a cut-off point, separating teams that survive from teams that do not. The difference becomes steadily less as the number of possible outcomes increases, because the graduations between them become smaller. Thus ranking exercises – apart from the suggestion just made – do not rate very highly on the winning/losing dimension because matching one list of ten against another list of ten allows very many possible outcomes. In card-sort exercises the situation is even worse, and discussion games do not really develop beyond judging solutions as 'better' or 'worse'. The programmed simulation and the maze rate highest, because the 'perfect' outcome (right choices at all points) is achievable, and where this does not happen an error-count is quickly and easily made.

THE EFFECT OF SUBJECT MATTER

A management training session normally has a known learning objective, which suggests appropriate subject matter. Despite the emphasis placed here on motivation and enjoyment, these are not ends in themselves and the subject matter should be examined to see whether presentation as a game is sensible. Game formats require that the material should be limited and should be fitted into a known structure, so thought must be given to matching format with subject.

DOES THE SUBJECT INVITE THE MAKING OF DECISIONS?

Few subjects cannot be presented so as to invite decisions, but the objective might make it inappropriate. If, for instance, a session was about the value of an open-minded approach, then to block off opportunities by concentration on mutually exclusive options would be wrong.

HOW EXTENSIVE IS THE SUBJECT MATTER?

Is the subject matter so extensive that, even when broken down into separate parts, it would be quite out of proportion to the limited information-handling capacity of a game? Games need clear, limited and stylized information. They cannot handle important issues that extend into several related areas and have no clear boundaries.

In these cases the only option is a serious, open-ended discussion exercise with few game-like characteristics.

CAN THE SUBJECT MATTER BE HANDLED IN STAGES?

Programmed simulations and mazes use successive decision/result stages which can be devoted to different issues. They do not work well if overloaded with information (the effort of understanding it all seems disproportionate to the limited choice mechanism) but it may be that a subject can be presented almost like an on-going story. Information for each stage is kept to a level the mechanism can handle, but what was absorbed for the first stage is still available for later stages, so the full picture gradually builds up in the minds of the players.

CAN THE SUBJECT MATTER BE DIVIDED BY ATTRIBUTES?

Is it possible to list component characteristics of the subject that contribute to its value, or applications to which it might be put, or points that distinguish it from other subjects? As soon as recognizable parts of the subject can be separated out, there is the material for a ranking exercise or a card-sort exercise. Which of these is used depends on the number of attributes discovered. Card-sort exercises can handle many attributes, while ranking exercises work well with small numbers.

EXAMINING EXISTING MATERIAL

The potential user of a management game can apply the reverse of this reasoning. He can look at the options allowed in a programmed simulation or a maze and ask whether these reasonably reflect the subject to be discussed. If they are very extensive, then perhaps an attempt has been made to squeeze too much material into a rigid structure. Similarly, in looking at the attributes used in a ranking exercise, it might appear that important items have been left out in the interests of making the exercise playable. In a card-sort exercise, it may be questioned whether all the attributes are genuine, and worth inclusion. If not, perhaps some padding has been added to make the exercise outwardly impressive. These are all questions about the match between subject matter and chosen vehicle. A good match suggests that the material will be acceptable to the players, arouse interest and motivation, and prove useful.

MATTERS OF DETAIL

Several passages in this chapter have emphasized comparatively small matters that are alleged to have a significant effect on player motivation. A particular case is illustrated in recent developments in the use of mazes. Earlier mazes were administered by numbered papers, with instructions like 'If you are choosing option 3, then take paper 17.' The game setting consisted of small teams gathered in corners of a room and a central table loaded with piles of paper. At intervals, team members rushed to the table and snatched up a paper. Today many mazes are in the form of computer programs, which is administratively much easier but may remove some of the game-like atmosphere that used to exist. The logic of the change is clear, but if one has accepted that some training activities depend upon people having an enjoyable experience then the logic is not compelling. The danger is greatest if responses are not printed out as hard copy but read on the screen, a temptingly convenient option. There are several drawbacks to this method:

FREEDOM

The earlier format allowed groups to choose where they sat and in what formation. The new format compels them to sit in a half-circle round a computer screen.

GROUP IDENTITY

The earlier format offered no focal point external to the group, so there was a sense of togetherness about the discussion. The new format makes the microcomputer dominant and tends to give extra power to one group member – the one sitting at the keyboard and able (in extreme cases) to make an entry before group agreement on the move. There is a tendency for people on the fringe of the group to lose interest.

ACTIVITY

The earlier format changed the physical formation of the group at each decision point. Somebody left the group to collect the new paper, and everybody else shifted and stretched at this well-defined break in the event. The new format involves no activity beyond the pressing of a key.

PROMINENCE

The earlier format made whichever member collected the chosen paper the focal person in the group for a brief moment when the others said 'Read it out to us'. The new format has everybody staring at the screen, reading at different speeds and perhaps interrupting one another.

COMPETITION

The earlier format involved some estimation of what competing groups were doing, because the papers they were picking up could be noticed. There was scope for some speculation and excitement, and comments like 'They took number 26. We haven't had that one, have we?' Under the new format each team exists in its own space capsule, huddled around the machine.

It may be preferable to have the microcomputer located away from the group, so that one member has to make a physical move each time, and to insist that he returns with the hard copy.

4 Games to increase group effectiveness

Many problems are tackled not by one person but by a cooperative group. Interested people bring their individual mix of knowledge, skills and abilities in the expectation that to put these together will reveal a good solution. Sadly, human groups are not always skilled at working together and outcomes are often imperfect. Management games can be used to improve group effectiveness in ways that relate both to knowledge and to behaviour. Common objectives include the following:

- To demonstrate the use and value of specific procedures, and to allow players to practise them. Methods of problem-solving and decision-making are covered, as well as committee procedures and disciplines intended to encourage creativity.
- To transform intellectual knowledge of how a group should work into observable results by increasing the interpersonal skills of group members.
- To help groups work effectively within a hierarchy, where there is normally an appointed leader who has personal responsibility for the outcome.

A useful general title for such games is problem-solving exercises, because the vast majority pose for the playing group a single problem (which can be of almost any type) and afterwards review the group experience to establish what happened, and why, and to draw out lessons. Before examining problem-solving exercises in detail, introductory exercises must be mentioned.

ICEBREAKERS

The first step in group formation is to become acquainted, and devices used for this purpose are commonly referred to as 'icebreakers'. They are quite short and present the group with a problem so structured that in order to solve it group members have to talk with each other. There might, for instance, be information shared out amongst the group and at successive meetings between two parties they would trade their 'personal' items of knowledge. In this way they would gradually acquire the total stock, and be able to piece together a message. Icebreakers have become an identifiable grouping and are available in 'collections'. Examples are *A compendium of Ice-breakers, Energizers and Introductions* edited by Andy Kirby, Gower, 1993 and *Ice-breakers. A sourcebook of Games, Exercises and Simulations* by Ken Jones, Kogan Page, 1991. Materials normally used for other purposes are sometimes pressed into service as icebreakers, but in that case their more complex elements are not pursued.

OBJECTIVES OF PROBLEM-SOLVING EXERCISES

When the range of material is wide and somewhat confusing, the clear specification of objectives is more important than ever. Once this has been achieved, the potential game user can ask and answer sequential questions such as these:

- What characteristics does my objective direct me to look for in an exercise?
- In which type of exercise are these characteristics most commonly found?
- Within that type, what exercises can I find that could be used as they stand, or used with a few changes?

The more common objectives of problem-solving exercises can be examined and to do so will bring some of these in-built characteristics to light.

IMPROVING THE DISCIPLINES AND PROCEDURES OF DECISION-MAKING

There is general agreement that decision-making is improved by following a consistent discipline, and several exercises to encourage this exist in the market-place. Here is a scheme using just five decision-making steps which interact with each other.

1. Reach a common understanding about objective and purpose.
   All members of a group should hold the same view about what they are trying to do, and why they are trying to do it.
2. Agree upon criteria of success.
   A group should look forward, imagine various possible outcomes, and decide which it would and would not regard as successful. This may reflect back on and modify the earlier step of reaching a common understanding.
3. Collect and analyse information
   There must be an open-minded search for relevant information, avoiding the narrow focus that so easily leads to useful ideas being ignored.
4. Develop alternative courses of action.
   It is essential to have more than one alternative. A single idea cannot be tested by comparison.
5. Compare the probable outcome of each course of action with the agreed success criteria.
   This is the point of decision. Applying the precept conscientiously will provide a ready answer to the question 'Which option do we choose?'

These steps form a logical process which can be objectively observed as a group tackles a problem-solving exercise. When the work has been completed, it is often possible to point out errors such as the following:

- Some members did not have the same idea as others about why they were trying to reach an objective. People who were looking at Purpose X, say, thought it was important and worked very hard. Others had Purpose Y fixed in their minds, which they saw as being of limited value, and this led to them making limited effort.
- Items of available information were not noticed or not properly used.
- Only one possible approach was seriously considered. There was, therefore, no comparison that could be used to probe its strengths and weaknesses.

A facilitator who wants to concentrate on this discipline would have to choose an exercise which gave an opportunity for the various steps to be attempted or omitted and performed well or badly. It would have to be so written that different understandings about the objective are reasonably possible, perhaps through ambiguity. Variations in the criteria of success would need to be possible, perhaps by making clear the need to avoid failure while leaving 'success' a vague concept in need of closer definition. The exercise would have to provide imperfect data, while hinting at the chance to gain more. It would have to permit more than one credible course of action, so that alternatives could be developed and compared. These are identifiable exercise features that can be looked for by the user.

IMPROVING THE DISCIPLINES AND PROCEDURES OF CREATIVE THINKING

Problem-solving exercises are sometimes used to stimulate creative thinking and this is seen as a plus factor in group work because it enlarges the number of options from which a choice can be made. Exercises can demonstrate the limits within which human beings typically think and can be used to encourage brainstorming. It seems strange that an undisciplined quality like creativity should be aided by the imposition of a disciplined procedure, but the intention is to suspend (for a specified period) the critical faculty that so often causes us to reject novel ideas unexamined. The discipline forces us to insert extra stages that can be called 'uncritical recording' and 'constructive examination', so that partially formed ideas escape rejection and live long enough to be modified, extended and made workable.

Exercises can emphasize the process of creative thinking and allow opportunities to practise it. The best known is perhaps the square made up of nine dots that must be joined together by just four, interconnected, straight lines. The need is for material that highlights a critical point and has few distracting issues. One source of such devices is *Imaginative Events* by Ken Jones (McGraw-Hill 1992).

IMPROVING THE DISCIPLINES AND PROCEDURES OF CONDUCTING MEETINGS

Despite increasing interpersonal skills, and the desire for consensus decision-making, many groups fall back on the imperfect but well understood rules of committee work, orderly debating and voting. These are legitimate, well-understood methods, and practising them is another sensible use for games and exercises. The material chosen must simulate the variety of objectives and attitudes and information that people bring to a real-life meeting.

INCREASING INTERPERSONAL SKILL

There are procedures a group should follow, but how well they are actually done depends on the interaction between members. Do they cooperate as well as they are able? Sometimes the answer is 'No', and the reason may be that non-cooperation is for the moment a more satisfying emotional response. Of course, this is not an openly declared reaction. No adult is going to say 'You've upset me, and I'm now going to ruin your game by taking my ball away'. Nobody can see into another person's mind, so provided one maintains outwardly respectable behaviour one can adopt that attitude mentally and remain fireproof. Nobody can prove your motivation.

We all seek approval and esteem and like to look good in the eyes of others: we decide how we are going to conduct ourselves in a group by a subconscious analysis of what is going to happen when we speak. Do we expect to be listened to and treated with respect and consideration? If so, we contribute freely. Do we expect to be ignored and contradicted and put down? If so, we keep our contribution to the minimum. We make up our minds about what is likely to happen by watching the behaviour of others: how each of them behaves towards us, and towards other group members. The rationale of having a group work on a problem rather than a single person is that the group brings variety and a range of opinions which are expected to enrich the final solution. If knowledge possessed by individual members is not shared, and if differing – even contradictory – opinions are not understood, then the purpose of assembling a group is lost. However, it does happen. We find groups in which individual members feel 'The effort of conveying my ideas is just not worth it. Every time I try, somebody responds with rudeness and aggression. Nobody even attempts to grasp my argument. From now on I will just keep quiet.' In this way, many valuable contributions may never enter the group discussion. For example:

- Values that would affect the determination of objective and purpose.
- Items of factual information that would alter the way people perceive the problem.
- Relevant experience and skill, which might change the group's evaluation of its overall capability.
- Creative ideas, which might enlarge the range of options under consideration.
- Logical arguments and criticisms, which might alter the group's judgement about alternatives.

Improvements in group process are likely to produce a 'climate' which is psychologically pleasant, in which members trust each other, and in which they will communicate freely.

The best problem-solving exercises contain critical elements which are easily overlooked or misinterpreted. Sometimes, when the 'right' answer is revealed, a group member will remark 'I thought it might be like that, but I did not speak up because. . .'. In such cases it is clear that the group failed to create the optimum problem-solving climate in which every potentially useful idea could be heard.

When the primary exercise objective is to study interpersonal skill one wants as much interaction as possible. Therefore necessary characteristics in an exercise are that everybody should be able to contribute and everybody should want to contribute. The latter point is less obvious than the first, but if several group members do not care what the group decides, then their contribution will be as little as if they had no relevant knowledge.

MAXIMIZING THE BENEFITS ASSOCIATED WITH LEADERSHIP

The suggestion is, then, that group effectiveness benefits from a range of defined, teachable, almost 'procedural' skills and also from interpersonal skills. The need for both sets is clear in a leader, and despite the attention currently given to maximum group cooperation and the 'empowerment' of individuals, most organizations still maintain a formal power structure. It is the appointed leader who finally has to account for all actions and who is the immediate recipient of praise or blame. Certain behaviours are expected of such a person:

- To act as a link and integrate the interests of group members and the organization.
- To understand and communicate the demands made of the group by the hierarchy, and the limits within which it must work.
- If the group cannot reach a consensus, to make a personal decision and accept the consequences.
- To ensure that, however it was reached, all members know what the decision was and what they are now required to do.

Many of these responsibilities can be simulated by the simple device of designating a leader and giving him full authority. A somewhat aggressive brief from the facilitator to the leader might be 'We are going to regard ourselves as operating within the confines of a traditional bureaucratic structure that is keen on efficiency and not too gentle with senior people. You are in charge of this unit. You are responsible for the results and you are very well paid. If the operation goes well, you may be promoted. If it goes badly, you may be sacked. Go ahead.'

A sometimes unappreciated effect of this device is that it effectively creates three stages of a hierarchy. The facilitator has become part of the simulation because it is he who delivers the brief. He is in the position of a senior manager passing an assignment down the line, and himself liable to error. Either by design, or by genuine accident, the facilitator may give an imperfect briefing and create the situation in which the 'leader' ought properly to press for clearer instructions before instructing his own staff. If desired, the facilitator can make such a situation worse by ungracious responses to questioning or by simply making himself unavailable. ('I have been summoned to a meeting in Frankfurt!')

An exercise to be used for this purpose would need to have a very clear outcome, so that the leader can be seen to have succeeded or failed. It would also have to be sufficiently complicated as to be beyond the competence of one person and ensure that the leader was dependent on his people – that he had to be truly a manager in the sense of achieving results through others and accepting personal responsibility for those results.

The objective–device link can be approached from the opposite angle. The next sections consider particular types of game/exercise to see what suggestions can be drawn from their particular characteristics.

RANKING EXERCISES

Ranking exercises, as referred to in another context in Chapter 3, provide players with a list of items (usually ten) and call for these to be sorted in order of importance. They owe much to the range originating in NASA, which postulates a group wrecked in a remote and dangerous location (the moon, the desert, the Arctic) having salvaged a limited number of usable items. Typically, each group member makes a personal rating, and then the group discusses the problem and reaches a consensus solution. This is then compared with an 'expert' solution. The solution prepared by group consensus should be closer to the expert solution than that of any single member and it can be claimed that the group has achieved some degree of synergy, i.e., the whole has proved better than the sum of its parts. Ranking exercises are so strongly associated with these 'survival' exercises that the terms are often treated as interchangeable, but 'ranking' refers to the method and 'survival' to the subject. Ranking exercises about other subjects are also available.

Ranking exercises are particularly suitable for the study of decision-making, allowing all appropriate steps to be illustrated. In many cases an expert answer is provided, with reasons why each item holds its place in the rank order. One can therefore look back on the decision-making process and see what was done well and what was done less well. For instance, if a shaving mirror has a high rating in the expert answer because it can be used for signalling, is that apparent in the group answer? If not, is it because nobody thought of it or is it because somebody *did* think of it but was not encouraged to speak? If the latter, then there has been poor decision-making at the collecting information stage.

Ranking exercises, especially the survival type, are also useful for studying interpersonal behaviour. They are about subjects on which few people are experts but which most people understand, so everybody can reasonably contribute. The dramatic nature of the simulated problem – a matter of life or death – usually ensures that people are interested and *want* to contribute. The exercise therefore benefits from the high level of involvement that supports the study of behaviour. There is plenty of activity for the observers to observe.

CARD-SORT EXERCISES

Card-sort exercises also require that items should be set in order of importance, or classified in some way. In one sense they are less effective than ranking exercises for the study of decision-making, for the individual decisions are less significant. However, this fact also works in the opposite direction, the relative unimportance of each individual card placement making it easy for potentially valuable comments to be suppressed. Group members who suspect that their views are in the minority, and expecting a critical reception, tend to ask themselves, before speaking, 'Is it worth the effort?' In card-sort exercises the change one is asking for (or sacrificing) seems quite small and people keep silent. This characteristic makes it interesting, after completion, to give the cards to the member apparently least committed and request 'Now show us how you would sort these cards if it was your sole responsibility.' Asking questions about that person's reasoning will often elicit important arguments that were not voiced in the general discussion, thus showing that the group was not successful in obtaining access to the full range of its members' ideas.

The card-sort format is specially useful when the decisions involve personal values, as for example, if a list of 'crimes against society' has to be sorted into grades of seriousness. Understanding and appreciating the value systems embraced by colleagues makes it easier to work amicably with them, bringing greater group effectiveness.

PUZZLES

'Puzzles' provides a convenient umbrella title for those games to which there is a single correct, almost mathematical solution. They range from short, apparently simple problems – like the nine dots and the four lines – to complex logic puzzles requiring deductive skill. A common form of the latter is 'Who owns/lives in/plays the fox/castle/piano?' The scenario describes a situation in which there are five groupings, each of them having one specific item from five generic groups. There is a list of clues which, followed through logically (and perhaps requiring several possible solutions to be tested) leads the participants to construct five correct lists. The clues are single-sentence statements like 'The labrador belongs to the man who plays skittles.' The exercise can be found in several places with a different subject and different words, but the same principle applies.

Some of the simpler puzzles are relevant to the creative thinking objective, and the more complex ones support training in decision-making and interpersonal skills. However, their in-built characteristics have a special effect in the two latter cases.

PRACTICE IN DECISION-MAKING

Puzzles usually provide a clear objective, so the decision-making stages of identifying 'What we are trying to do?', 'Why we are trying to do it?' and 'What we will regard as success?' do not exist. The other stages are present, but the absence of these early stages is a weakness.

RESTRICTED INTERACTION

A marked characteristic of puzzles is the need to follow through a logical train of thought. This needs persistent attention to *one* line of attack rather than a quick survey of many options. It is well suited to a single person working alone, or a small group – not more than three – who share a detailed understanding of the line they are following. It is not a process well served by the interjection of alternative ideas at uncontrolled intervals. The general interaction that supports the study of interpersonal behaviour is therefore less frequently seen in puzzles. Sometimes the only contribution that can be made by somebody not totally familiar with the present state of progress is 'Let *me* try!'

A CONCENTRATION ON GROUP MAINTENANCE

The fact that puzzles favour solution by small groups can be turned to account by deliberately using them with larger numbers. The frustration aroused then brings an excellent opportunity to study the concept of maintenance. 'Maintenance' refers to the processes by which individual group members obtain sufficient psychological reward from membership that they remain keen and committed. There is an exact analogy with the maintenance of a machine: if bearings are not oiled they seize up, and if people find an environment unrewarding they leave. In one sense it can be argued that the human case is the worse one, for people may 'leave' only in a mental sense – continuing to take the money but contributing minimally. It may even be unclear whether they have 'left'.

Complex puzzles exercises can create an erratic pattern. Progress gives way to frustration; frustration is overcome; one idea fails; another is introduced; the energy that is driving the group comes first from one person and then another. Each individual feels excited and depressed by turn and makes more or less effort. There are excellent opportunities for examining the causes of personal feelings and their effects.

If such an exercise is used with an appointed leader, the problem of ensuring that all group members are gaining some satisfaction (or even noticing whether they are) can be extremely taxing. Even if forewarned, the leader may be unable to answer post-event questions like 'Which of your members do you think received most enjoyment from this activity, and which was most discontent?'

COMMUNICATION GAMES

To label an exercise a communication game raises once more the difficulty of classifying management games. Almost every device could be called a communication game, for almost every one depends on the communicative process. Some games overtly set out to study communication; others make no mention of it at all but make good communication such a determinant of success or failure that communication game seems the only sensible title. Some commonly found types are listed below:

- Games that focus on accurate description and the limitations of the spoken word.
  Participants may be asked to describe a set of geometric shapes to someone else who then draws them. These can be single stage exercises, or can be run, first, with one-way communication, and then with questioning allowed – to show improvement.
- Games showing the need for preparation and planning of communication.
  These are rather more elaborate, perhaps providing data about the communicative circumstances as well as the subject matter. Participants must not only consider how to 'transmit' clearly, but also assess how the listener is likely to interpret the communication, and adjust their strategy accordingly. There is a significant overlap with negotiating exercises.
- Games about the psychological aspects of communication.
  One reason for communication failure is simply that people do not bother to attempt it, feeling that the climate is too unfavourable. Some games set up such situations by choosing a controversial subject which will arouse partisan feelings and the probability of a majority/minority split.
- Games about the organizational aspects of communication.
  Some games simulate two or three levels of management, perhaps emphasizing the problems of a hierarchy by inserting restrictions on inter-level communication.
- Games about the cultural aspects of communication.
  By establishing different communicative rules in different groups, and causing people to move between them, the experience of working in a foreign culture can be simulated.

OTHER CLASSIFICATIONS

Two other classifications that might be distinguished are initiative tests and searches. Individuals or small groups are sometimes asked to perform unusual or bizarre tasks which demand interaction with non-related parties who may or may not have been forewarned. The idea has something in common with the military practice of dumping soldiers in an unkown location miles from their barracks and requiring them to find their way home with very limited resources. Such exercises sometimes work well, but can also cause embarrassment and confusion. The task 'bake a loaf of bread' has been used successfully in a friendly rural hotel: it would hardly work in a city-centre venue.

Searches or hunts are also popular. They may be scavenger hunts, treasure hunts with clues, or spy-style events with two parts of a message written on the halves of a torn postcard. They can be useful in examining how thoroughly a group thinks through a problem and how the personalities interact. Even amongst senior managers, there is likely to be one member who is less patient than the others, who insists on dashing off in search of a clue, and is thereafter out of contact with his colleagues, to the disadvantage of them all.

UNIQUE MATERIAL

It will now be apparent that defining types of game solves only some of the problems. It enables one to recognize an accepted title and know broadly what mechanism that game employs, and to make judgements based on the known strengths and weaknesses of that mechanism. However, it does not help to assess the material that, sometimes because of its richness, has no more specific title than 'problem-solving exercise' or 'decision-making exercise'. These must be investigated individually to discover what happens when they are actually played.

In that connection, it helps to ask the question 'What situation does this exercise simulate?' It further helps to apply that question not to the *subject* or *environment* of the exercise but to the *player behaviour* it is expected to produce. For example, it is possible to categorize an exercise by saying:

> 'It sets up a situation in which success depends upon all the group members interpreting the task in exactly the same way.'
>
> 'It sets up a situation in which critical items of information – from separate sources – have to be recognized and matched.'
>
> 'It sets up a situation in which failure to apply the highest quality standards will mean certain failure.'

These are quite different questions from 'What product or service will the players be talking about?' That sort of question has its own relevance, but does not help to understand the basic nature of an exercise.

THE EFFECTS OF INDIVIDUAL USE

The situation is further complicated by the fact that changes in the way an exercise is used may make it appear, and be described, in a totally different way. A few examples are useful.

FOUR-LETTER WORDS

The Gower exercise, Four-Letter Words requires a group 'to make four letter words from the letters in that (closed) box'. This instruction is of course ambiguous, and without effective communication it can happen that two people take differing courses of action, neither having realized that his own interpretation of the words is not the only interpretation possible. If the user emphasizes this feature then it is a communication exercise. Once participants have agreed on an interpretation, there are several credible ways to organize the group and it becomes a problem-solving exercise or a decision-making exercise.

EXERCISE PROSPECT

The game Exercise Prospect is a board-and-counters game in the treasure hunt form. The single clue is ambiguous, and unless group members discuss what it means they are likely to pursue different strategies based on different premises. Thus it is a communication exercise. However, the exercise has a clue, and that clue can be turned into a key which will bring success. Thus it is a puzzle that one can get right or wrong.

PERCEPTIONS

In the exercise Perceptions from Wessex Training Services the task is to apply certain logical rules to a number of patterns and distinguish between those that do and do not qualify for a special title. It is quite complex, and can fairly be called a logic puzzle. An excellent additional use of the exercise is to make group success dependent on successful use of the agreed identification logic *by one group member, selected by the facilitator*, i.e. that member is tested. This means that those in the group who fully understand the method must communicate very well to those who do not, and ensure that the latter will themselves be able to communicate convincingly if the choice falls on them. The main feature has now become communicative skill.

In many cases, the skilled user can gain more from an exercise than at first sight appears to be built into it. The key to recognizing potential lies in the point made earlier about categorizing skills and situations in general terms, and using general descriptions about behaviour. Which skill do you want people to have a chance to practise? Can an exercise create a situation in which that skill is critical to a good result?

5 Games about organizations

A more complex area of study than individual behaviour and the behaviour of cooperative groups is the integration of groups or functions as they form subsystems of an organization. The need to study behaviour is still present, and some of the exercises used still employ an abstract background, but there is also a powerful tradition of simulating specific situations and specific organizational systems. These have a significant knowledge content.

SIMULATION

The unqualified title 'simulation' is used as the least unsatisfactory of several possible terms. From one viewpoint, every device in the whole field could be described as a simulation and it is invidious to use the word for one group only. Yet many of the other devices can be clearly identified by more specific titles. Thus 'computer simulation' has been used for one well-defined category, and 'board game' has been used for games that, despite being simulations, have the board as their most obvious feature. Likewise 'role-play' is sometimes used as a title despite the fact that role-plays are often simulations. The devices that do not have some well-accepted alternative title might be given a new label like 'system simulation', but it seems artificial. The method adopted here is to use 'simulation' and to follow it, where possible, with a statement of the means by which the simulation is carried forward.

Simulations are hard to classify because each of them has developed in a pragmatic fashion. They have no common root except the desire to do better than just 'tell people'. The originator of a simulation starts from a position like this:

- 'I wish I could *show* them what it's actually like.'
- 'I wish I could help them to feel what it's like.'
- 'I wish I could give them the experience of being a part of it.'
- 'I wish I could give them a chance to practise'.
- 'I wish we all shared a common understanding of what it's like, so that our discussion could be deeper.'

The next step is to ask whether the real situation can itself be used for training. If it cannot, then perhaps something akin to it, something having similar characteristics, will prove an adequate substitute. But how much of the original situation should be simulated? Which characteristics must be included and which can be left out? Must the simulation be visibly similar to the real-world activity (like the quintain) or is it enough to focus on, say, particular skills required in the real-world activity? One might, for instance, decide that the skill most needing improvement is 'recognizing and interpreting precise details'. In this case the device would properly be described as 'simulating a situation where success depends on attention to the details'. The outward appearance might be nothing like the activity towards which the training was directed. This is a critical choice, because creating outward similarity is restrictive: one is starting from a single image of a well-defined activity and the less the simulation looks like the reality the less effective it will, by one standard, seem to be. By contrast, a simulation designed to increase a particular skill can use any situation in which that skill is relevant. This gives the simulation designer much wider limits.

The great variety of objectives, boundaries and methods makes the search for suitable material amongst what already exists a frustrating task. There are so many unknowns. The most useful advice is still rather general. Certainly, the enquirer should take the following steps:

- Define clearly in his own mind what it is that he wants to simulate. Is it a specific situation or is it an example of a general situation? How much of the situation has to be simulated?
- Consider what sort of people are going to use it, and their cultural orientation. (Later comment will emphasize the fact that there are differences in what will be found credible by different groups.)
- Examine the material with an open mind, being specially careful not to reject items merely on account of some non-relevant title. The *method* of simulation is something quite distinct from the *subject* to which the method is applied. A simulation that is described as being about a totally foreign activity may prove to have a method that transfers perfectly with a few changes of terminology.
- Acquire as much familiarity as possible with methods of simulation in general, and face the fact that building one's own simulation may be the best option.

Given the high degree of variety in the subject, this chapter sets out to:

1. Describe some simulations, and the purposes for which they are used.
2. Show some of the methods employed, with their strengths and weaknesses.
3. Show some of the ways in which quite simple changes can increase the applicability of a simulation.

One all-pervasive characteristic of human systems is speech: people talk to each other. The easiest way to replicate a situation off-the-job is therefore to use role-play. With this as the starting point, one can see what happens when the imagined situation becomes too complex to be handled by memory alone. One can see how techniques of representation are brought in, and sometimes aspects of reality itself.

SIMULATING ENCOUNTERS THROUGH ROLE-PLAY

If one wants to simulate an encounter between, say, a job applicant and an interviewer, the spoken word is often enough. There is an obvious likeness, here, to exercises used for other purposes, and the same situation might be used to study an interpersonal skill like listening. What turns it into a simple type of simulation is the assignment of specific roles, which carry their own responsibilities and their own assumptions about appearance, objective and correct behaviour. Suppose that two people were assigned roles as car salesman and potential customer. The salesman would need listening skill to discover what the customer wants, but he would also need characteristics of the specific role, such as product knowledge. If such a role-play were moved from a lecture room to a car park it would become one degree closer to a real simulation and would show some of the benefits of introducing *things* as well as *words*. For instance, it would be possible to observe the salesman's degree of skill in noticing and using to his advantage the particular vehicles around him. An extra dimension would have been added.

The value of role play can be increased by stimulating disciplined comment from non-participants by giving them an observer's brief. Such a brief might read as follows.

Here are some good and bad behaviours commonly seen in sales interviews. Whenever you see the salesman behave in one of these ways, make a mark against it.

1. Listens carefully to customer.
2. Shows by his reply that he has heard what the customer said, and understood.
3. Asks questions about the customer's needs.
4. Interrupts the customer.
5. Demonstrates that he has extensive knowledge of the product.
6. Allows the customer time to think.
7. Gives an evasive answer to a question.
8. Reacts angrily to any criticism of the product.
9. Makes derogatory comments about competitive products.

Any one-to-one encounter can be simulated, but most often used are those known to be critical, such as buyer and seller, union official and manager, superior and subordinate, and applicant and recruiter. At one time role-play was unstructured and imaginative role-players destroyed the exercise by inventing whatever background would justify their performance. Today, practitioners take trouble to provide a credible environment so that the action remains within known boundaries. One device is to prepare written briefs for the parties, each referring to the same situation but describing it as the particular party sees it.

Role-plays (and other games) can be video-recorded and played back for analysis and discussion. However, it is a time-consuming activity and not always justifiable.

SIMULATING A MEETING BY ROLE-PLAY

The concept of written briefs can be employed to set up simulated meetings in which participants demonstrate some of the problems of organizational life.

One of the purposes of formal meetings is to share the knowledge and information available from departments and to hammer out an agreed policy that all will be able to implement. Within each department people naturally attach high importance to their assigned departmental goals and are relatively ignorant and uncaring about those of other departments. This is natural, since they neither have influence over, nor responsibility for the actions of other departments. This situation can be simulated by asking small groups to consider the departmental 'angle' on a given problem and to prepare a brief for one member who is going to role-play their departmental head at a meeting. Thus several people sit round a table, all with different objectives (to promote the views of their department) but also sharing the common objective of reaching a workable solution from the viewpoint of the organization. If and when some solution is reached, the departmental heads can be returned to their departments to 'sell' the solution to those who work for them. This type of simulation is full of lessons about why conflicts arise in organizations, and what can be done about them.

This format also reveals a common problem of simulation – that where a person has a unique role it becomes the centre of his attention and diminishes his interest in what is happening elsewhere. And there are always 'star parts' and 'bit parts' so that learning opportunities can be uneven. In the simulation described above, imagine five departments of five members each, only one of whom can role-play the departmental head. This leaves twenty people who can only observe. It may be a useful experience for them, but it will not be the same as the experience of the person who is out in the middle rejoicing when he makes a telling point and sorrowing when he makes an error.

The issue is discussed here because simulations are sometimes mounted to add their special strength to certain specific messages. In this exercise it is possible that the chosen departmental head might (in his real-life persona) be noted for criticism of his boss for failure to 'fight his corner'. Being in an identical position, and finding out personally just how difficult the representative role is, might be very illuminating. But the experiential value is for that person only: for others it is an academic observation. A necessary consideration before using such a simulation is therefore 'What benefit will the whole group receive from it?' It may not be justifiable to mount an elaborate exercise that offers deep experience to a few people. There is also the fact that such elaborate role plays can be satisfying to the organizer when they have 'gone well'. It can be tempting to stage them without thinking through the objectives and the alternatives.

There are, of course, compromise solutions. One (in the context of the exercise described) is to have more than one meeting of departmental heads. If the departmental teams were six strong, there could be three meetings in parallel, each attended by departmental heads plus observers. More people are involved and there are useful comparisons to be made, but detailed debriefing of three sessions becomes impossible.

SIMULATING A CUSTOMER/SUPPLIER INTERFACE

An example which illustrates how careful identification of the process to be simulated can affect the structure and detail of the simulation is the customer/supplier interface. Several teams of 'suppliers' are required to call in turn upon an equal number of potential customers. Thus Team 1 calls on Customer 1 while Team 2 is with Customer 2, and then they all move round. The critical question is the nature and purpose of the interview being simulated. If the calling team is expected to make a sale, then there has to be quite elaborate data about the product itself and about the customers' circumstances, and care must be taken to ensure some degree of consistent response from the role-played customers. Further, shall the product be one that the role-playing suppliers sell in real life or shall it be something different? If the former, the simulation may become side-tracked by experience-based arguments about what would 'really' happen. If the latter, each role-player must assimilate the data provided and make interpretations which cannot easily be judged right or wrong. These are surmountable problems, but they demand extra work and they reflect the uncertainty that often attaches to role play.

An alternative definition of the purpose of the interview is to become acquainted and build a relationship. This follows the belief that in an era when competitive products offer little inherent advantage over each other, customers often buy from the supplier with whom they feel comfortable – the one whose people they like and trust and with whom they can communicate. Thus the supplier teams are not expected to sell anything, but rather to find out about the customer and present themselves (and their company) as 'good people to do business with'. Using this scenario, most of the difficulties mentioned above have vanished because only very limited briefs are necessary. The supplier brief can be as short as: 'For Interview No. 3 *your* firm sells cars and *his* firm has a large team of representatives selling cosmetics through hairdressing salons'.

A SIMULATION AND A GAME

The customer/supplier simulation can acquire game characteristics by requiring each role-playing customer to judge the performance of each supplier as good, reasonable or poor. For each judgement the customer has an appropriate sealed envelope containing separate letters of the alphabet which he hands over after the interview, but without disclosing his judgement to the supplier. Back at their work stations, teams have a display board showing the message 'XXXXXXX is at XXXXXXXX suffering from XXXXXX'. The game instructions state that the blanks have to be filled in with the name of a member of the royal family, the name of a royal residence, and the name of an illness. The letters in the envelopes are so arranged that a team which receives consistently 'good' ratings will obtain the letters C, B, A, A, M, L, A, H, S, E, A, L, H, O, T, S, L, R, A, R, M and will be able to complete the message correctly. A team with some 'poor' ratings might finish with a number of inconvenient Xs and Qs and Ys. A successful team can display CHARLES is at BALMORAL suffering from ASTHMA.

The enjoyment of this variation is increased by the ingenuity of players who do not have quite the right letters but are able to make up deviant and humorous displays.

CHANGING THE FEATURES OF A SIMULATION

The same simulation, originally a role-play, can also become a simulation of a different sort. This is achieved by defining the product as something ordered and delivered quite frequently, providing symbols to represent it, and costs to the supplier. The brief to the role-playing customers is altered, requiring them to keep an up-to-date record of which supplier they would buy from if required to place an immediate order. The brief to the supplier is altered, requiring him to provide each customer with a current price list. At predetermined intervals, the facilitator passes a 'buying instruction' to a customer who then places an order. The scope of the simulation has now widened, because the supplier teams have to control their own stock position and balance costs of stockholding against the risk of becoming unreliable suppliers. They also have the pricing problems associated with the presence of competitors and an unknown sales volume.

SIMULATION OF A HIERARCHY BY ROLE-PLAY

The situation to be simulated can also be a characteristic of organizations in general rather than a part or the whole of a specific organization. One example is an exercise called Hierarchy. This is more than just a role-play, as it involves a task (making words) that can be judged by observation to be a success or a failure. It is based on several sets of small cards which carry letters or numbers in different colours. The exercise sets up a 'top level' group, a 'first level' group and a 'worker' group, which are geographically separate and allowed to communicate only through written messages. Unless there is good communication, it is impossible for the worker group to be sure what they are supposed to do. The briefs to the groups are written in a way that allows (without deliberately encouraging it) the introduction of inaccurate ideas about status and 'appropriate behaviour'. Players frequently generate such a poor communicative climate that the objectives are never reached.

A similar exercise in packaged form is Don't ask me, I only work here! from Gower. The product here is a simple ornament made from two fabricated cardboard cubes.

This simulator mechanism is convenient rather than realistic, and it does not simulate the total functioning of any organization. It selects and uses abstract representation, but it illustrates some of the problems that are associated with rigid hierarchies, geographical separation and perceived differences of status.

ROLE-PLAY AUGMENTED BY VISIBLE SYMBOLS

Simulations sometimes make use of physical materials because the original intent was to reproduce a specific, physical situation. These examples, however, show that materials can be there for a different reason – as part of the organic growth of a device. Role-play relies on the spoken word, and does not always guarantee what will result. The spoken word can be denied, disregarded, or rendered valueless by arguments about interpretation or differences in circumstances. And sometimes the imagined situation can become so complex that without a visual representation people lose track of it. So displays, tokens, records and physical objects become a part of the role-play for purely functional reasons. They are necessary. Hierarchy, for instance, encompasses a visible representation of the work through the arranging of letters into words. Don't ask me, I only work here! uses cardboard ornaments. Where forms of representation are needed to serve a purpose, and do the job effectively, it does not matter if they look like playthings. The Irrigation Game and The Green Revolution Game both use picture tokens (people, plants, sacks of fertilizer) to carry forward serious and valuable simulations.

SIMULATING A STATE OF DISADVANTAGE

Among the exercises aimed at understanding emotional states is Slow Learner, a simulation originated by Don Thatcher and June Robinson. This involves the imposition upon willing participants of artificial disabilities like poor sight and limited hand movements. In this disabled state the participants are told how to perform various tasks and are supervised unsympathetically while they attempt them. It dramatically increases one's understanding of the handicapped condition.

SIMULATING FUTURES BY ROLE-PLAY

One of the less frequent uses of role-play is to break free of the constraints imposed by formal behaviour and to encourage imagination. This is an extension of the brainstorming concept, in which time is given to voicing and recording novel ideas, however strange and impracticable they may seem. The difference is that people adopt specific roles and focus attention on the behaviour and objectives that accompany that role. The ordinary roles of the organization can be used, or the roles of competing organizations, or of customers or suppliers. One then receives comments like:

> 'Well, if you were to do *that* then my response would certainly be XYZ!'

The concept looks, and is, ludicrously simple, but it causes people to think thoughts that they would not think within the structure of a formal meeting with an agenda, minutes, and set objectives and prescribed forms of behaviour – procedures that, if departed from, attract unfavourable notice.

SIMULATION WITH PAPER AND PENCIL

A factory simulation used by Dr Anastasia Bukova uses as its product 'magic squares' as shown in Figure 5.1. The raw material brought into the factory is a piece of paper with a blank grid, and the 'work' is completion of the boxes with numbers, in such a way that the totals across each line, down each column and across the diagonals are all equal. A 'factory' is set up by a group of students, some of them occupying management roles and some of them writing numbers into squares. This simulation produces realistic activities such as the following:

- Training 'workers' so that they know what is required of them.
- Estimating the average time that will be taken to work out a set of numbers (all the Magic Squares produced must be different) and to write them neatly in the boxes.
- Deciding the price that will be asked for them, given data about material costs, labour costs and overheads.
- Negotiating with the customer (a staff member).

16	2	3	13
5	11	10	8
9	7	6	12
4	14	15	1

Figure 5.1 A magic square

- Setting production priorities, should there be a need for different sized products. (Such as a five-by-five square instead of four-by-four.)
- Inspection of completed work and rectification if appropriate.

Given the right participant group this exercise provides a very good cost/benefit rating. It is easy to set up, raw material is no problem and the only machinery needed is a pencil and a rubber for each operative plus a few calculators. It needs only a limited time allocation, so even if a participant has an unexciting role, that role will not last long. However, there are many opportunities for the sort of mistake that results from ignorance or lack of care and which is so salutary for the learning process. When such mistakes are made, the real-life parallel is clear, and the message stands out 'If we can make that sort of mistake in a simple simulation like this, how much easier must it be to make a mistake in a more complex environment and what care and discipline must be needed to avoid it.'

Magic Squares, which represents production equipment only by a pencil, can be compared with Paper Hats and with the simulation described below (Paper Booklets) that uses office equipment such as staplers and punches. They reveal different levels of realism. An equipment failure in Magic Squares can only be simulated by removing a workers pencil. In Paper Hats it can be simulated by removing the scissors (a bit more dramatic). In Paper Booklets it can be achieved by jamming a screwdriver into the jaws of a hole-punch (more dramatic again). In all cases the message is present, but the emotional impact of that message is likely to vary with the type of person in the student role. Highly intellectual people, accustomed to thinking in abstract terms, will be quite happy with Magic Squares. They may see pushing screwdrivers into paper punches as crude and unnecessary when the message is perfectly obvious anyway. Experience-oriented foremen from a traditional industry may find it difficult to see the relevance of Magic Squares but be delighted with the 'realism' of the disabled paper punch. One of the dimensions to be considered when choosing, or creating or adapting a simulation, therefore, is the nature and attitude of the participants.

SIMULATING THE COMPLEXITY OF MACHINE-BASED PRODUCTION

In the Paper Booklets' simulation, sheets of paper are cut to specified sizes and made up into booklets of so many sheets held together by a set number of staples, each inserted at a prescribed position. The booklet is then punched with a specified number of holes at precise positions. This is a realistic simulation in which some of the actions required of participants (like the use of production control documents) can be similar to those they would have to take in real life. All the demands of the Magic Squares exercise are there, plus the following:

- Timing and costing of machine operations.
- Calculation and costing of materials when less than the whole of the purchased item can be used.

- Control of the factory process when multiple operations are being undertaken.
- Reporting of any defects on work-in-progress.

As with other simulations, new features can be added. The following would all be possible:

- Purchasing problems
  They can be simulated by choosing a form of raw material that varies in quality, is hard to get, or comes only in inconvenient quantities.
- Choice of manufacturing plant
  Participants can be despatched to research the cost and effectiveness of various stapling machines and hole punches.
- Credit control and cash flow
  The exercise can be provided with its own currency, so that goods delivered have to be paid for, and if too much credit is allowed the firm experiences cash flow problems and cannot buy materials.

Although this simulation has wider scope than Magic Squares it cannot be described as 'better'. That depends on the purpose for which each is being used and the circumstances in which it is run. Paper Booklets is richer in content, but it takes time and energy to set up. Magic Squares is elegant and economic, but deals with a narrower range of issues. Paper Booklets works well with production people in traditional industries, while Magic Squares is more productive with university graduates.

The point was made in connection with an elaborate role-play, that powerful lessons for a few must be balanced against the time and commitment of the whole group. In Paper Booklets, an order can be fed into the factory that requires (if correctly interpreted) a staple to be placed in one position, and then a hole to be driven straight through it. If this order, which ought to be queried, is put through without comment it will provided a powerful lesson in planning to the operator who faces the final crisis. It is the sort of dramatic event that causes one to be impressed by an exercise, but it has to be remembered that only one person experiences the moment of drama.

SIMULATING PLANNING AND PROGRESS

The planning process requires looking into the future, making judgements about what is likely to happen, and providing sensibly for it. When students have attempted this sort of simulation, one wants to be able to ask and answer questions like:

- 'Did they (the planners) accurately identify the objective towards which their plans were directed?'
- 'Did they notice all the indicators on which estimates of the future might be based?'

- 'Did they evaluate all those indicators, and make a judgement about the likelihood of various results happening?'
- 'Did they project themselves into the future and consider the sequence in which actions would have to be taken, which resources would be needed at what time, and so on?'
- 'Did they examine what money would have to be paid out at what time, and when revenue would be received? Did they forecast their cash flow?'
- 'Did they examine any 'what if' scenarios, creating imaginary crises for themselves and discussing how they would react?'

Charts and documents are real-world tools for planning projects and controlling their progress, and can themselves be used to simulate an imaginary situation. Such a simulation becomes more dramatic and effective when there is a physical structure to be seen. Dramatic scenarios may result, for example:

- With game time scaled to represent real time, it becomes obvious that the structure is not going to be ready by the promised date.
- Reluctance to order parts far enough in advance brings work to a halt. People sit around doing nothing until the facilitator releases some component.
- The completed structure fails the specified physical test.
- It can be shown that the completed structure does not comply with the design specifications.

This case can be used to answer the question 'Why bother with physical simulation?' It could be argued that the objective was fully achievable by players preparing plans on a standard document, the facilitator announcing progress in accordance with a script, and the players showing their response by amendments to their plans. Why use physical representation instead? The dramatic aspects provide one answer, but another lies in the fact that the physical components are more specific. Suppose, for instance, that a critical feature of a project was availability at the right moment of a particular electrical switch box. In a paper exercise a facilitator who says 'You haven't got it' might be told 'Of course we have. It is covered by this entry here (pointing to a document) about ordering supplies.' If the simulation has a physical element, and a supplier has to hand over a physical object under proper conditions of notice and payment, then there can be no argument. Errors and omissions can be denied or belittled where there is no specific evidence that they have taken place. A physical element provides firm evidence and throws doubt on the comment 'Of course, in real life we would never forget an item like that when we were actually talking to the supplier!'

SIMULATION OF RELATED GROUPS

An organizational problem of great interest today is the relationship between different departments. Traditional bureaucratic practice separates one department from another and, by assigning specific responsibilities, also creates some inclination not to cross boundaries – to leave other people to get on with 'their' work while we get on with 'ours'. A greater desire to see an organization working as a single cooperative team, and making use of all the skills and abilities of its people, has forced a new look at bureaucratic structures and a desire to make them work better. An interesting simulation directed to this end is Sister-Teams, an exercise which sets up three departments, linked only by telephone, and gives each of them apparently quite different tasks. The fact not known to the playing teams is that some of the tasks, though described in different terms, are complementary. Thus one group is required to arrange certain words (printed on separate plastic strips) into a meaningful pattern while another team has a crossword puzzle. What neither team knows is that the words on the plastic strips are the answers to the crossword, while the location of the words in the puzzle is the answer to the pattern problem. Traditional communication between departments is fairly superficial and deals only with matters of obvious common interest – and at that level the dialogue is likely to be 'We have a crossword puzzle. You have some plastic strips. Oh well, Good Luck. Goodbye!' Only if they talk in greater depth – if they take some genuine interest in each other's problems – do they realize the cooperative opportunity that exists.

THE BEHAVIOURAL ASPECT

The descriptions given show that most simulations have a substantial knowledge content but, because the participants are personally involved, they also invite the study of process issues. They allow examination of interaction between the people and how they feel about their situation. The objectives set by the user of the simulation will determine which receives most attention, but both aspects are there, and both are valuable. For instance, the hierarchical exercise can be examined from a theoretical viewpoint asking the question 'What can we learn from this about the dangers inherent within hierarchical organization?' It can also be used at an emotional level asking the question 'What does it feel like to be ignored and kept in ignorance? What attitude does it generate in you?'

6 Model-based business games

Model-based business games were developed in business schools and universities, using the concept of economic modelling. Players receive a description of an imaginary business and an imaginary environment and make decisions – on price, advertising, production targets, etc. – about how their company should be run. The decisions are compared with a model, which determines how well they have fared. A 'model' in this sense is just a set of mathematical rules which state that if a certain decision is taken then a certain result will follow. The detail of the rules is not made known to the players. The simplest example of such a rule is a price/demand relationship establishing a sales demand figure (X) for every possible asking price (Y). A model of this sort can be very simple or very complex. The term 'model-based' is generally used to describe games that have a repetitive decision/result cycle moving onward through time – each cycle represents a certain length of real time, such as a month, a quarter or a year. The players' decisions establish the policies to be followed during that period, and the results are 'what happened as a result of them'.

Models are also core features of other types of game, but in this type – named for them – they have special prominence. Players submit their decisions to the same model time after time: it's presence is ubiquitous. The games are written in such a way that success is partly dependent on making sound commercial decisions, but there is also the opportunity to make deductions about how the model behaves and to gain limited skill in manipulating it.

MANUALLY-OPERATED BUSINESS GAMES

In a manually-operated business game the consequences of the team decisions are worked out by an administrator (or umpire) using a set of written rules and basic technology like paper and pencil, graphs, or a hand calculator. They allow only limited complexity and sometimes appear a poor relation to the impressive devices requiring a microcomputer. Nevertheless they have many advantages.

A CLEAR IDENTITY

The very simplicity of these games identifies them as exercise material intended for learning purposes. The more complex games invite argument about how real and accurate they are, leading players to spend too much time judging the quality of the model and not enough on the messages it is intended to convey. A manually operated game is unpretentious and arouses no such attitude. It is clearly not intended to be totally real, and the fact bothers nobody.

LEARNING OPPORTUNITIES

The clear, simple lessons of a manually operated game can be thoroughly understood, making it easier to concentrate on how they should be applied. This is not the case if one plays a more complex game and finishes it somewhat confused. It is very easy when choosing or creating a game to be seduced by the concept of realism and end up with something that is too difficult and which the players never fully understand. Since players are being asked to enter an imaginary situation and are not aware how the model has been written, the playing experience can be quite testing even when the model from the umpire's point of view seems ridiculously simple. It is wrong to believe that a manually operated game is by definition too simple to offer a good learning experience.

INDEPENDENCE AND CONFIDENCE

For users not experienced with the microcomputer, manually operated games may be popular as they do not force reliance upon external sources. Provided the user is prepared to study the material beforehand and practise, and can do simple mathematics, nothing much can go wrong. By contrast, dealing with computers from a position of weakness is fraught with problems. Equipment proves to be unavailable or is locked away; software fails to match hardware; expert advisers mumble unintelligible gibberish; the screen displays incomprehensible jargon instead of the desired answer.

ABILITY TO EXPLAIN

A further great advantage of a manually-operated model is that the facilitator knows how each result was worked out and can give convincing answers to aggrieved questions. Such questions are an inevitable feature of business games – people receive unwelcome results and want to know how these can be justified. With a manual model the facilitator can help. With a computer controlled model most facilitators have at some time been forced into responses like 'I don't know' or 'That's what the computer says and you will have to live with it.'

CLEAR LEARNING POINTS

The relative simplicity of the manual game combines with the repetitive decision/result cycle to produce a very effective learning method. It is possible to concentrate on a small number of critical decisions and progress through the experience of getting them wrong, learning why they are wrong, and then getting them right. This feature is less marked in complex games because one's attention is spread over a wider field.

AN EXAMPLE OF A MANUALLY-OPERATED GAME

The following example illustrates the way manually-operated games work and some of the features that need special attention.

DESCRIPTION AND DATA

So that players can make reasoned decisions there has to be a description of the imaginary situation and a certain amount of data. The description enables players to visualize the environment and make common sense deductions about what sort of results are likely to happen. The data fills in details and gives clues about the numbers that might be appropriate. The extent of the description and the data is always a matter of concern, for providing too little means that players feel they are being asked to make wild guesses, while providing too much entails reading a thick, demotivating package of paper before any action can be taken.

The game Lawn Trimmers postulates several companies manufacturing a product and selling it through retailers. The market is described as segmented according to price so that there are five brackets. The story-line is that potential customers take the price tag as an indication of quality and accordingly view the product as of high or low quality. The jargon word for this is a convention.

CONVENTIONS

A convention is a way of massaging reality so that it can be made into a playable game. It equates with the attitude 'We know this is not quite true, but we will accept it in order to make things work'. Business games are full of conventions, and they are generally well accepted by players provided they are explained and understood. The most obvious convention of all is the separation of on-going business activity into discrete time periods.

In the example of Lawn Trimmers, the convention allows the establishment of five price brackets within which the teams must set their price to the public. This makes a start on the problem of game boundaries.

BOUNDARIES

A game situation is by definition imaginary and therefore the vast stock of commonly known facts from the real world are suspect. Players do not automatically know what is ridiculous and what is not, and the game papers cannot possibly tell them everything. There is always uncertainty, and teams sometimes hand in decisions which the model judges harshly despite the fact that the team has made no culpable error. It may be that it has made a reasonable assumption that just did not fit in with the game designer's concept. So boundaries have to be indicated in some way. Prices, for instance, can be suggested by giving upper and lower limits within which they must lie. Another way to indicate boundaries is to set up a game so that teams take over an existing company and receive copies of 'the last set of decisions/results before the old management team was fired'. The data can be fixed so that the previous decision was poor: it thus offers an exciting chance to turn the company round while also giving some indication of what constitutes a sensible set of decisions.

There is not in fact a 'warm start' in Lawn Trimmers. The teams are invited to set up a factory, which may be small, medium or large. A table lists the cost of each factory, the highest and lowest quantities that can be made in it, and the unit cost of making the product at any given volume of throughput. This goes a bit further than just setting boundaries and makes a start on the idea of encouraging reasoned decisions.

ENCOURAGING REASONED DECISIONS

Games decisions are always based on a mixture of facts and assumptions. If only facts were used then games would be nothing more than exercises in mathematics. If only assumptions were used they would just be guessing games. When there is a suitable mixture, the teams can exercise skill in noticing and analysing the factual data, deciding what it means, and using it to help frame their assumptions. As well as the production data already referred to, Lawn Trimmers provides data about the market size in each segment and the number of teams competing in it. It is therefore possible to make rough calculations about the level of sales possible in each sector and match this with the establishment of a suitable factory. Sensible examination of the data reveals that it would be a great mistake to set up a large factory and then enter the most expensive market segment. The factory is only economic when producing a high volume and the most expensive market segment is that with the lowest volume of sales. The inevitable element of guesswork attached to the first cycle of a game is thus limited by the chance to base important decisions upon logical analysis of facts.

AN UMPIRING MODEL

The model used to umpire Lawn Trimmers is operable by paper and pencil without even a calculator. There is a separate set of rules for each market segment, and in each of these there is a base figure for sales demand which reflects the overall sales volume of the segment. It applies whatever decisions are made. Onto this base figure the umpire adds extra units for:

- Every percentage point of 'margin' allowed to the retailer through which the goods are sold.
- Every month of guarantee offered with the product.
- Every £1,000 of advertising.
- Every £1 by which the price is below the allowed top price for the market segment.

The number of units to be added for each of these variables is different in each segment. Thus retail margin matters a great deal in the most expensive segment because retailers will be selling fewer items. It matters less in the lower segments because higher sales volume compensates for a reduction in unit margin.

This is an example of a model so simple that the skilled umpire can produce an answer for a team decision in less than a minute. It uses the convention of market segmentation and it further uses a base figure for sales demand that applies irrespective of the other decisions. In theory this could lead to the ridiculous situation of a team winning sales when – despite the fact that the product is only sold through retailers – they set the retailers' margin at zero. It does not happen: the text of the game makes clear that a margin is expected and, anyway, the level of the base figures is too low to allow profitable operation using such a strategy.

Another method of manual operation is a nomograph. That illustrated in Figure 6.1 embodies the manually-operated model for a game about marketing caravans. In that game, players are asked to assume the role of Marketing Director and make quantitative decisions about advertising expenditure and number of sales centres and number of models. They write these on a pre-printed decision form and hand it to an umpire or 'facilitator'. Assume that one team decided on £6,000 for advertising, 4 sales centres and 7 models (meaning types of caravan), the user of the nomograph would draw a horizontal line across the page on the £6,000 level and mark the place where it crossed the curve marked 4 centres. From this point he would draw a line to the mark on the lower horizontal scale for 7 models. He would then read off sales value from the higher of the two horizontal scales, obtaining a figure of about £220,000 for sales value.

OUTPUTS OF AN UMPIRING MODEL

Neither of the two umpiring models described tell the playing teams their 'bottom line' in terms of financial performance. They have to calculate it for themselves. The reason

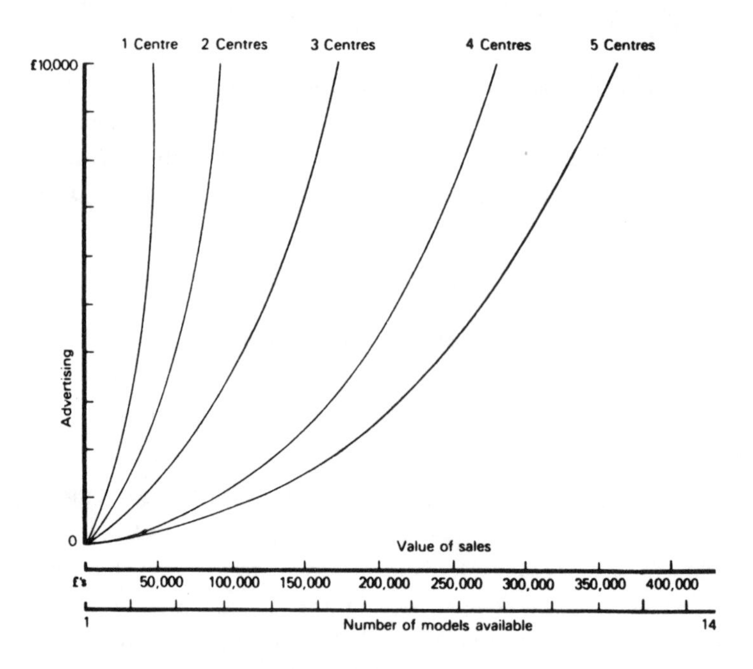

Figure 6.1 A nomograph

for this is mainly that umpiring is essential for those factors that are concealed from the players but not so for subsequent calculations. The post-umpiring calculations include matters such as the following:

- Have we enough goods to meet the demand? What money are we going to get in for these sales?
- What stock have we got left over? What will be the total stockholding charge?
- What are our total costs and what is our profit?
- How should our profit/loss account and balance sheet read?

In computer-based games the results can easily be provided in 'final' form such as profit/loss account and balance sheet, but there are still valid arguments for not doing so. The user who goes straight to the bottom line will quickly find cases where students learn less rather than more because they are unable to see how the final documents have been built up and therefore do not recognize the connection between their earlier decisions and the results that they see. This is another case where clear identification of the objective and clear analysis of the learning need are important. Players who do not know how to convert 'raw' data into financial terms will benefit from being forced to do so. Players who are familiar with the necessary steps will find it boring.

From the facilitator's point of view a problem in making players work out their accounts is that they may do it incorrectly. It is embarrassing to find that the apparent winners of a game have got their sums wrong and are really at the bottom of the league.

THE MEANING OF INTERACTION

Simple games also offer the easiest demonstration of the interactive process. Consider an umpiring device that takes into account price, advertising and number of salespeople employed. The output of this device can be treated not as a measure of actual sales to be returned directly to the players but as a measure of the effectiveness of their strategy. This can be compared with that of the other teams in order to establish percentage shares of a market.

Assume four teams whose strategy effectiveness measures are 2,600 (Team A), 4,300 (Team B), 1,500 (Team C) and 4,700 (Team D). Added together these total 13,100. Assume also that the umpire's rules relate total market to total of strategy effectiveness indexes (TSEI). The result might be:

TSEI of 13,100 = total market of 95,000 units.

An interactive game would require this total of 95,000 units to be broken down between the four teams in proportion to their individual strategy indexes. The outcome is shown in Table 6.1.

Now suppose that in the next decision period Team C improved its strategy to achieve an index of 2,750, while none of the other teams made a change. The TSEI would then be 14,350 and the percentages would be 18, 30, 19 and 33. Assume that the rules for calculating total market give:

TSEI of 14,350 = total market of 97,000 units.

The result would now appear as shown in Table 6.2.

Teams A, B and D have suffered a downturn in their sales that is not attributable to their own actions. If, using this simple model, teams were not made aware of the decisions and results of competitors, working out what had happened and why would be quite a puzzle. And if they were given all the figures it might still be a problem,

Team	*Strategy index*	*% of TSEI (and market share)*	*Units sold*
A	2,600	20	19,000
B	4,300	33	31,350
C	1,500	11	10,450
D	4,700	36	34,200

Table 6.1 Interaction of team strategies – example 1

Team	*Strategy index*	*% of TSEI (and market share)*	*Units sold*
A	2,600	18	17,460
B	4,300	30	29,100
C	2,750	19	18,430
D	4,700	33	32,010

Table 6.2 Interaction of team strategies – example 2

because they might find that Team C had changed all three variables, so it was not clear which change had improved its index most. If more than one team had made changes, then the problem would be worse still. This reinforces the idea that a model may be unsophisticated from the viewpoint of the umpire, but obscure even to intelligent analytical players. Very few people working through these games as players can make more than approximate statements afterwards about how the model works.

It is with interactive, manually-operated games that the turn-round time of umpiring is most likely to be a problem. However, the method of achieving interaction described above is not the only means available. An alternative is to calculate strategy effectiveness indexes and use these to create a moving average against which to judge each new decision. This means that each team can be umpired whenever it is ready. It is affected by the average strength of recent strategies, and its own strategy contributes to the strength that the next team will encounter.

THE MECHANISTIC STRUCTURE OF MODEL-BASED GAMES

Manually-operated devices, because of their simplicity, show very clearly the heavy dependence of model-based games upon variables that can be expressed in numbers and upon economic rationality. This is a well-recognized characteristic, and must always be taken into account when assessing the suitability of such games, and their manner of use.

7 Computer-controlled games

The previous chapter discussed some simple model-based games which do not require computer support, though it may sometimes be convenient. This chapter considers games that do need computer support. A good starting point is to look at national and international competitions.

COMPETITION FORMAT

It is sometimes thought that games used for national competitions are extremely complex. This is not wholly true, for the playing teams come from many different levels in many different organizations, including schools. As far as complexity is needed to sort the good from the very good, and determine a winner, it is achieved by altering the environment in successive rounds so that it becomes steadily more difficult to handle. John Handley, General Manager of the Cranfield School of Management, which runs the National Management Game from Cranfield, makes the point that in such a game the most critical characteristic is that performance criteria should be clear and unambiguous. The basic format of such games is quite well defined.

1. There is often a sponsoring company, allowing entry fees to be kept at a reasonable level.
2. The competition is advertised to a target population, which may or may not be limited by type or geographical location. The advertising will probably specify that the game will be played in so many cycles, over a period of weeks or months. For the early rounds, it will be conducted by post, but there will probably be a final at a central location. The competition will be invested with a certain prestige and worthwhile prizes will be offered.
3. Within eligible institutions, interested people form a team under the banner of their school, company, division, or professional association. This is entirely voluntary, and the team members meet for several hours in their own time at intervals within the game decision periods.
4. The game documentation will describe the state of the imaginary company, so

that all teams take over an organization that is in the same competitive state as the others. There will be information about the business environment, its history, and perhaps some forecasts about the future. This information can be used with more or less skill and may be in writing, or as a data bank on a computer disk.

5. The decisions required by the teams will be mainly quantitative decisions, requiring values to be set. One such game has forty-four variables. Another has sixty-three. Increasingly, the subjects about which decisions are required will be wider than simple production and marketing decisions. There is likely to be an international element, allowing different prices in different markets and gains or losses due to currency fluctuations. There may be decisions about use of the company's cash resources, involving imvestment and portfolio management. There may also be qualitative decisions about company policy, especially on environmental matters.
6. The teams may be encouraged to make 'what if' projections in order to assess possible consequences of alternative policies. This can be achieved by directing their attention to commonly available spreadsheets, or by providing them with a game-specific program on disk.
7. Decisions are usually written on forms and sent by post or by fax. Direct computer link is not yet practicable because the teams are likely to have different facilities.
8. Depending on the number of entries, the teams will be grouped so that they compete directly with only a limited number of other teams. They will not know the real-world identities of these teams.
9. The computer model will be an interactive model in which the market is influenced by predetermined trends (or on-going decisions by the administrators) and by the behaviour of the playing teams themselves. The term used by Cranfield School of Management for this format is Team Interactive, as opposed to Model Play games in which teams play separately against the computer.
10. 'Feedback' will be in the form of operating statements and financial statements. It will be accompanied by up-dates about the market situation, and by whatever market research has been requested and paid for on the decision form.
11. At some stage the less successful teams will drop out, though this misfortune is sometimes mitigated by a 'plate' competition for first-round losers. Successive drop-out stages follow until an appropriate number of teams are left for the final event. This will take place at an up-market location with prestigious attention from the sponsors and the media.

INTERACTIVE GAME OR NON-INTERACTIVE SIMULATION?

Not all games used for competition purposes are interactive in the sense described in Chapter 6, for it is still a competition if teams compare their performance against a common standard. In this case all teams play the same game, but do so independently and win or lose depending on the fiancial result. In a survey of games used for competitions, Cranfield School of Management found a fairly even split between the two types.

The great advantages of the non-interactive simulation, for the ordinary user, are convenience and clarity. There is no need for different teams to play in a synchronized manner, which makes a significant administrative difference. And the absence of uncontrollable competitors makes it much easier to tease out logical connections between the decisions a team has made and the consequences they subsequently experience. In a business context this can be viewed as unrealistic and therefore a weakness, but only in relation to certain objectives. For others it is entirely acceptable. When examining systems that do not feature direct competition between like and like, non-interactive simulations are specially valuable. They handle natural systems well, and are excellent for exploring environmental relationships and ecosystems. Examples of such simulations are Fish Banks Ltd and the Mahakali Simulation (irrigated agriculture).

Between simple games and national competitions is a wide range of material suitable for in-house use: either by buying a packaged game or by using external consultants. The differences between them are best examined by starting from the users viewpoint and considering the critical variables of objective, playing group and time.

GAME OBJECTIVES

By far the most important consideration in choosing and using games is precise identification of the objective. The potential user ought to be asking 'What am I trying to achieve?' The question has to be pursued thoroughly, because superficial answers like 'helping people to learn about business' are not enough. What business are they supposed to be learning about? What aspects of it matter most? Is there a precise learning objective at all? The answers naturally affect the device that ought to be chosen. Possible reasons for running a computer-controlled business game are considered below.

TO EXPERIMENT

A person who has no previous experience of the method might want to discover how well it works in his situation. The risk involved here is that players will be committed for a long time to something they do not understand (or see as irrelevant) or which breaks down in chaos. It would make sense to choose a game with a background relevant to the playing group, relatively short, and easy to administer computer-wise. It would make no sense at all to use an extensive, complex game.

TO DEMONSTRATE THE TOTAL BUSINESS CONCEPT

Another requirement might be to create awareness amongst people with rather narrow experience of the total scope of business operations. So the full range of activity, from obtaining supplies to paying dividends, would have to be featured and the game chosen would be a reasonably complex one. Would it matter that the level of complexity prevented full understanding? This is where the identification of objectives is important, for 'awareness' does not imply full competence and it may be quite enough that the playing group should go away with, for example, a new appreciation that somewhere beyond their immediate environment are people called shareholders. They will also have realized that these people need to be satisfied and are actually rather important to the continued existence of the company.

TO ENCOURAGE STRATEGIC THINKING

Strategic thinking is the antithesis of the traditional attitude that concentrated upon continuation of an accepted historical activity. Strategic thinking concerns looking forward, anticipating the state of the market and the moves of competitors, setting long term goals, and working steadily towards them. Because they stretch forward in time, and because of their interactive capability, business games are potentially valuable for encouraging this approach. The objective automatically specifies some of the game characteristics needed. It must *not* be a game that impedes players' progress with minor details about present operations. It *must* be one that projects a fluid and competitive environment extending years rather than months into the future. It may, perhaps, feature competing companies that are *not* (as most games assume them to be) exact replicas of each other.

TO FULLY UNDERSTAND PARTICULAR PHENOMENA

Another objective might be to give players an in-depth understanding of a few subjects: an understanding so thorough that it influences their daily decision-making. This calls for a game that puts heavy emphasis on a few characteristics, which might mean that it does *not* simulate all aspects of business activity. Some operations might be deliberately omitted to highlight the central relationships and prevent the attention of players being diverted to 'non-essentials'. Thus the device sought will not be a total simulation. An example of an activity that might be omitted because it is not immediately relevant to the objective is raising capital and rewarding it through dividend policy. This constitutes a homogeneous subject area which can be inside the simulation or outside, depending on need.

How complex does the game need to be? People will not be able to utilize concepts unless they have a proper understanding of them, so the game must be designed so that before it ends, players 'get it right', recognize how they have achieved this, and feel able to do it again. For this sort of objective a game that sends people away with 'awareness' rather than comprehension is not enough. It has to offer clear, comprehensible messages and for that reason the most complex type of game is unsuitable. One can usefully ask, when looking for a game for a specific case 'Is there a secret of success?' Answers might be 'Effective control of cash flow', 'Never sell below marginal cost', or 'Pay attention to customer requirements'. These answers indicate a game directed towards a specific and clearly identified learning objective.

COMPETITION, TEAMBUILDING, ENJOYMENT

These objectives are more connected with what happens between the players than with what they learn about a specific subject. Indications are that the game should be complex because anything appearing too easy has two significant drawbacks. It is not challenging, and it is unable to separate the good team from the very good team. It does not matter that nobody achieves complete understanding of what is taking place, provided they are not totally lost either. The state of mind in which players say 'We *think* the most important variable is X, but we are not certain' is excellent: a little uncertainty contributes to enjoyment.

PLAYING GROUPS

Computer-controlled business games are an intellectual activity, dealing with the imaginary and the abstract. The more complex games are not suitable for players unaccustomed to thinking in abstract terms. Given players who do think that way, complex games are quite acceptable but demand an extra time allocation whenever there is a shortage of subject knowledge. School sixth forms, for example, have little trouble with the concepts and procedures of business games but are unlikely to know about price/earnings ratios and so on. Excessive time spent explaining new ideas is an interference with the playing experience, so a relationship between knowledge level and acceptable complexity certainly exists. Also, to learn about a subject merely to play a game is rather pointless. The expected learning must have some perceived relevance.

Playing groups also reveal different levels of motivation, and here one must be careful not to be over-influenced by the keenness and dedication shown by players in the national competitions. Entrants for these are entirely self-motivated: they actively want to take part; they are aware of what they are letting themselves in for; they also retain control of place and time, for within the time schedules of the playing periods they can meet when and where they like. In-house training programmes may be quite different. Attendance is not always voluntary, the time and place are fixed and there may be critical attitudes based on feelings like 'I don't need this' or 'I can't spare the time' or 'I am afraid I shall do badly and that somebody important will notice it.'

TIME

The in-house situation is often constrained by limited time. The entrants to open competitions commit themselves voluntarily to the activity, and in educational institutions time allocations are made by the teaching staff. By contrast, as an in-house training specialist is beset by demands to limit 'unproductive' time. Time, that is, that could allegedly be better spent calling on customers or earning revenue in some direct manner. Games that need a long time to play, or require extensive reading, are impracticable. One device on the market is supported by an instruction manual of 100 pages. Not many in-house training specialists could rely on course participants to undertake that much preparatory reading.

ISSUES OF COMPLEXITY AND REALISM

The user who has asked and answered questions about objective, playing group and time is better prepared to consider the issues of complexity and realism.

COMPLEXITY

First, what does complexity mean, and is there any way of judging a game before playing it? There are certain factual indicators.

1 Number of decisions to be made in each time period

Almost all business games operate by equating a certain length of playing time to a certain length of real time, and requiring – in every such period – decisions about a certain number of subjects. These are commonly called decision variables. Traditionally they were written on a decision form and passed to an umpire. It remains a convenient title even though some games now have no decision form as such and operate by keyboard entry of data.

How many items are on the decision form? The Lawn Trimmers exercise in Chapter 6 does not need computer control: its decision form has four variables. Towards the other extreme is Topaz from Edit 515 Ltd. This is not the most complex of their games but is a suitable example because it is publicly available under licence. There are about sixty items on the decision form. Clearly, a model handling sixty variables is more complex than one handling four.

2 Length of instructions

Business games are intended to be about judgement, not guesswork. To ensure this, there must be data: data which can be assimilated and interpreted with greater or less skill. The more decisions there are, the more data is needed, and therefore a greater volume of explanatory text. Lawn Trimmers has eight pages: Topaz has twenty-five.

3 Time requirement

The more detailed a game, the more time players require to make sensible decisions, and the greater the number of decision periods that can be sustained before interest wanes. Lawn trimmers has a suggested playing time of two to four hours. The suggested allocation for Topaz is eight playing periods of two hours each, totalling sixteen hours in all.

This comparison makes it obvious that the two games are intended to address different objectives and to be used in different circumstances.

REALISM

Realism and complexity are clearly connected. Business is at times extremely complex and this encourages the assumption that a complex simulation is necessarily a realistic simulation, and that a realistic simulation is by definition good. This conceals a number of fallacies.

1 Business is always complex

It is not. Some businesses are relatively simple to run, and there are some simple principles that have universal application. One basic lesson that can be learnt without any computer technology is the old accountants' adage 'Turnover is vanity: profit is sanity.' Some players have emerged from complex business games with less real learning than could be achieved by ten minutes reflection on this saying.

Realism is necessarily good

It is not. This idea relates to the question of objectives, and the possibility that a game may be intended to promote understanding of a particular area. It may then be deliberately *unreal* – an exaggeration of certain features, almost a cartoon. Another distinction is between the inculcation of specific behaviour patterns, to be reproduced in real life, and the understanding of principles, which can be applied to differing circumstances with judgement and discretion. The objective is the criterion. It would be unsatisfactory to train aircraft pilots by using a simulator of an aircraft they were not going to fly, because the inference of that training environment is that 'You do in here what you are later going to do out there.' If the same inference was part of the business game environment then exact realism would be important. Generally speaking that is *not* the inference. The more likely one is 'Here are some phenomena whose general behaviour you ought to understand.'

An illuminating comment – taken from an early draft of The Nottingham University Economics Department Business Game – is this: 'Such games are not usually designed to replicate exactly the world of business but serve instead to simulate a range of problems commonly encountered in commercial activities.'

In the context of business games 'realism' is often equated with 'accurate numbers'. Ken Peattie of Cardiff Business School, writing in MANAGEMENT EDUCATION AND DEVELOPMENT, makes a fair criticism of computer simulations in that they may perpetuate 'a sort of planning by numbers philosophy'. He describes an approach to teaching business strategy which uses fantasy role-play as a way to encourage people to think about objectives, strengths and weaknesses by *comparative study at a general level.* This is realism of a different type from that commonly assumed in business game discussions.

3 Increased realism can never be bad

If one accepts that realism is not always good – that it can sometimes be a distraction – then it becomes possible to envisage a situation in which increased realism actually makes things worse.

4 The new capabilities associated with computer technology are always going to bring improvements

The train of thought here is: 'Business games are complex – computers can cope with complexity – therefore computers are good for business games.' They can certainly cope with complexity, but one is often lured into using that capability just because it exists. The following cycle has been acted out several times:

1. Computer technology makes it possible to create a simulated situation that is more real, in some dimension, than before.
2. It becomes important to embrace and use this technique in order to appear credible.
3. Somebody discovers that the learning objective (as distinct from the objective of realistic modelling) can be achieved equally well, and much more economically by a quite different method.
4. The use of the computer is reassessed. The valuable aspects are retained and those that the machine has improperly usurped are handled by traditional methods.

Repetitive though we know it to be, only by working through this learning cycle can the best methods be found. Presumably something similar will happen when 'virtual reality' is introduced to the training world.

FOR WHAT USES IS THE COMPUTER APPROPRIATE?

There was a time when computer-based material was prestigious and high-profile. It almost guaranteed a good reception and 'rave' notices from students because of its novelty value. The novelty element has now largely disappeared and the disadvantages of microcomputers are visible. People who do not like playing with computers are not afraid to say so, and those who like them are sometimes so experienced that they are critical of what is presented to them. The user must always ask 'Do I actually need the computer? Is it doing anything that could not be done better and cheaper by some other method?'. What then are the strengths and weaknesses of the computer?

The following comments are specially relevant to direct-access games, in which each team (or sometimes each player) has a microcomputer.

ADVANTAGES

1 It can make projections

Human beings can make statements about the future. They can say what influences they believe will exist, what they plan to do themselves, and what they think their competitors will do. They can even make quantitative plans. What they cannot do within a reasonable time frame is work out the mathematics of the complex relationships they have postulated. The computer can. It can accept multiple decisions from many different sources and say 'As a result of what you have all done (and the assumptions programmed into me), this is the new situation.' To have that complex, elaborate mixing process carried out is a great advantage. It provides an objective result with which one can compare one's hopes and expectations. It enables one to identify critical interactions that one would otherwise not have been appreciated.

An interesting use of this facility is the type of game in which players make what might be called 'administrative' decisions about an imaginary company as well as 'policy' decisions in the old sense of price, number of salesmen, advertising budget and so on. It is possible in this type of game to make decisions about the structure of an organization, succession planning, or the delineation of territories. These are assessed by the program and make the imaginary business 'fitter' or less fit to pursue the business plan laid down by the quantitative 'policy' decisions.

2 It does things quickly

Demanding more calculations is not the only possible response to the computer's ability to calculate quickly. Sometimes the speed can be an advantage in itself because it removes a delay that would prove boring and demotivating. This sort of benefit can be seen in the games from Winkler Marketing where teams make decisions about a limited number of critical marketing variables so that the entries for each team are quite short – just a few figures – and the computer rapidly displays comparative measures of volume, income, costs and profit for *all* the teams. There is nothing complex about these calculations, but to do them manually would be tedious.

A similar effect is achieved by using a microcomputer to assess correlations with the 'expert answer' in a ranking exercise. Assigning priorities on the screen can be immediately followed by a display of results.

3 It can provide information and it can communicate

An ordinary microcomputer with a single disk can display substantial quantities of game-relevant data, provided the data has been built-in beforehand. Players can sit at the microcomputer and call up data about past performance, staff records, plant layout, maintenance costs, or anything else thought necessary. As one moves upwards into networking, very extensive capabilities become available. One can search linked databases of many types, send messages to competitors, suppliers and customers and call up reports from staff. In fact current technology would permit an almost perfect match between a game-player sitting at a computer and a real-life managing director – provided one could be found who communicated only in this remote manner.

Marco Polo is a networked game in which players operate in real time. They can be first or last to make changes in the market-place. They can share research facilities. They can buy or sell to each other. The method obviously has great potential.

4 It can provide control

If necessary, microcomputers can be programmed to keep track of time and obey predetermined rules about what is to happen at any particular moment or in any particular circumstance. In this manner they can reduce the administrative load on a game user.

5 It can amuse and entertain

The use of graphics, cartoons and icons means that computer screens can be a source of pleasure, and can contribute to student motivation.

DISADVANTAGES

There are some disadvantages to using the computer which are not always apparent to those who are familiar with the technology, but which are highly relevant for training and development specialists.

1 User knowledge

Both game user and machine operator (if not the same person) need some expertise to keep the system running, and even at times to make basic keyboard entries. In direct access games much time is wasted while people learn how to use the machine, or people who believe they know how to use it discover that the program is written in an unexpected manner. The ultimate disaster is a power cut.

2 Computers are divisive

Computers split the world into those who can handle them and those who cannot. If a game team contains both sorts of people, the former are likely to have an undue influence and reduce the motivation felt by the latter.

3 Computers control things

Because a computer will only accept interaction on its own terms, it is often seen as a malignant, controlling influence that interferes with human freedom.

BENEFITS OF COMPLEXITY

Given that complexity is not pursued for its own sake, or used in the wrong circumstances, there is much to be said in its favour.

1 Emotional impact

When a complex environment is realistically simulated, a great feeling of interest and excitement is generated. People gain a real understanding of what it is like to be in a top decision-making post, the variety of the problems one must handle, and the effect of working constantly in an environment of uncertainty.

2 Status

A residual feeling of second-best sometimes attaches to things that are 'not real'. To be provided with something that is real and complex suggests that trouble and expense have been accepted, and that it is appropriate to make such an investment for the people currently being asked to play the game.

3 Credibility

In so far as success in the game is supposed to relate to real-life success, a realistic model is more convincing than a fabricated one. The latter provides the emotional escape route of 'It was an unreal situation anyway.' If the quality of the game is such that it is clearly *not* unrealistic then this argument cannot be used and one takes one's inadequacies more seriously.

4 Construction

In one respect it is easier to create a realistic model than a theoretical one, for the reality one is modelling is there to be studied. Once the model has been built, it can be tested against known real-world behaviour. By contrast, the game constructed to demonstrate special phenomena, and using artifical data, has nothing with which to be compared. This may not be too important for the less complex games, but to create an extensive business environment that is wholly imaginary but internally consistent would be very hard.

This chapter has tended towards the theme 'On the one hand THIS, and on the other hand THAT'. It might cause the inexperienced user to feel that computer-controlled business games should be left well alone. Such a conclusion would be unfortunate. Most of the comments relate to the objectives and circumstances of a training/development session, and if a potential user bears these in mind it will be possible to maximize the chances of success. But computer-controlled games are sometimes recommended with great enthusiasm, and enthusiasts don't always emphasize the down-side of their wares. The potential user who has done some homework about the subject will have a more informed dialogue with the enthusiasts, and get better value from what they can offer.

8 Game use and game variations

This chapter offers ideas about maximizing the benefits of model-based business games, including computer-controlled games. It continues with a review of currently favoured 'options' – variations on the traditional form of a repetitive decision-result cycle.

CHOICE

Several comments have already been made on the absolute need to decide what one is using a game for: what one expects to gain from it. If that has been done, then the appropriate subject matter, scope, level and complexity of the game will have become apparent. A few additional considerations relate to the culture of the organization and the people who will be playing.

- Should it be a game, in which teams interact competitively with each other, or should it be a simulation, with an opportunity to analyse 'uncontaminated' data? The former environment is richer: the latter is more clinical.
- Should the computer be the focal point of the game, with teams making use of their own machine, or should the focus be on discussion round a table, the administrator receiving decisions and returning print-outs without a noticeable computer presence?
- Should the game be run without tutorial guidance, so that players must extract all the learning value themselves, or does the culture prefer that there should be some direct intervention – some 'telling' to back up the learning opportunities?
- Is it necessary to draw constant parallels between 'the business in the game' and 'our own business' or can players be trusted to perceive the likenesses for themselves?
- Is there any danger that a numerate, financial and mathematical emphasis in the game will be demotivating to people with lesser skill in these areas? Should some qualitative features be added?

PERSONAL PREPARATION

The user of a game must become familiar with the material beforehand and identify any characteristics that may cause difficulty. With a package this need is fairly obvious. One should work through at least one cycle as a player, and operate the umpiring process. Even where the game is being run by a consultant, the user should insist on being 'walked through' a cycle. Games are complicated and there is scope for misunderstanding between the user, who knows very little, and the consultant, to whom the details of the game are obvious and hardly worth mentioning.

Preparation is specially necessary with regard to computer equipment, which is full of shocks for the uninitiated. It is not enough to be promised by technicians that the equipment will work. Every piece of equipment must be tested in the conditions that will exist during play. Typical of the difficulties encountered is that training staff are often left with a mixed bag of equipment: a test on one microcomputer may prove quite satisfactory, but when the program is loaded onto other machines the screen picture is poor.

Is is also necessary to ask whether the playing group is familiar with the type of game to be used, or with other types. Earlier references have been made to different game traditions, and this means that people sometimes assemble 'to play a business game' with divergent ideas about what is going to happen.

PRELIMINARY WORK BY PLAYERS

Reference has already been made to the existence of preliminary descriptive information that must be grasped before players can become effective. What can be done to facilitate this process and bring players to the start-line well prepared?

PRIOR READING

This is an obvious strategy, which pays off if players have the opportunity and the will to do it. Where either of these is absent (a very common situation) the result will be that a few people have studied the papers but the majority will have just about read the title. The speed of the exercise will be determined by those who have not studied it, and nothing will have been gained.

A PRELIMINARY TASK

It may be possible to stimulate study of the text by requiring teams, or individual players, to undertake some investigative task that must be presented at the first session. This might be, for example 'Prepare a brief report on the market in which your company is going to trade.' Another strategy is to make one person responsible for preliminary study and instruct him to guide his team through the first session. Annoyance at his apparent dominance will spur the rest of the team to catch up fast.

VARIETY AND DESIGN

This may not be possible if consultancy services are bought in, but assimilation of data is made easier by the use of more than one medium and by good design. The thick wads of paper referred to earlier can be much improved by better layout, by pictures, diagrams and the use of colour. These changes may seem an unnecessary effort when the facts are undoubtedly present in word form, but society is becoming more visually oriented and attention spans may be short. It does make a difference if the reading of words is sometimes exchanged for another activity like interpreting a diagram. Figure 8.1, for example, shows the strategic relationship of competing firms in a market: it saves a lot of words. Information can also be made available on computer screens, thus adding further variety.

INTRODUCING THE GAME – MOTIVATION

Player response to a business game can be improved by understanding motivational principles and acting in accordance with them. The argument starts with the suggestion that learning is such a very obvious 'good' that one may easily overestimate its power and assume that the supposed outcome of the game – learning – will generate total commitment throughout. The truth about business games is that they run for quite a long time, may require much hard work, and are not *guaranteed* to produce the hoped-for benefit. So the game player is being asked to trade a considerable investment *now* for a *possible* later benefit. The investment may even be painful, in terms of the following:

- Giving up time that one would rather use another way.
- Undertaking tasks that one is not good at, and perhaps displaying inadequacy in front of others.
- Accepting a team role, when one would rather make independent, unilateral decisions.
- Cooperating with people whom one has not chosen and may not specially like.
- Experiencing frustration and failure.

The commitment of the potential game player can be regarded as dependent on a balance of expected cost versus expected benefit. If cost exceeds benefit, then the outcome is non-attendance or, if attendance is compulsory, a low level of commitment. If the reverse is true, then commitment is high. The game administrator naturally wants to influence this equation to gain maximum benefit, and there are just two possible strategies:

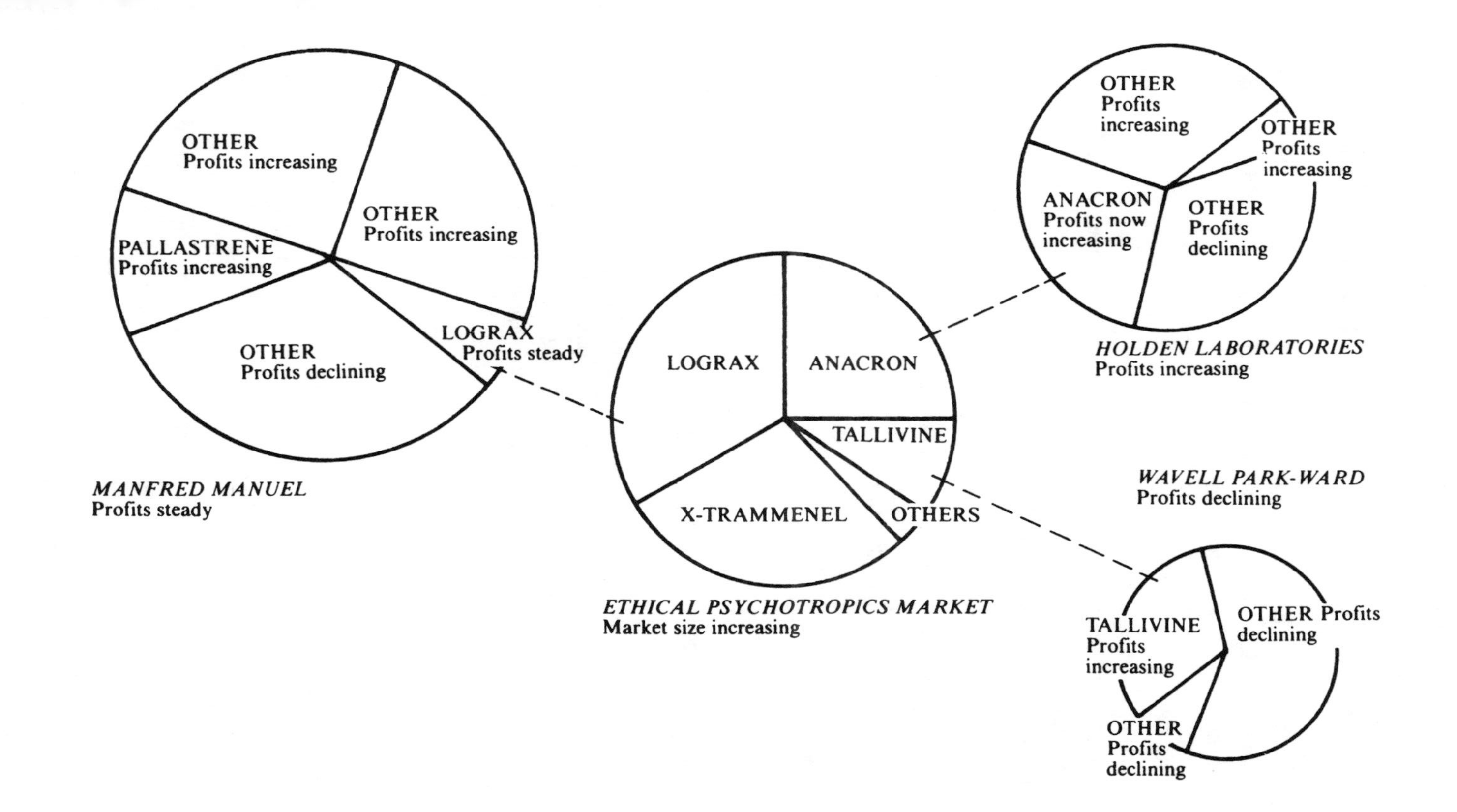

Figure 8.1 Graphic example of company relationships

1. Increase the perceived benefits, and/or:
2. Decrease the expected pain.

The best way to achieve both these objectives is to make the activity itself enjoyable and rewarding, so that the player does not depend on deferred motivation (the expectation of a reward to be received *later*) but experiences concurrent motivation through the psychological rewards received as he works. These rewards may take a number of well-established forms, for example:

- Perceiving the relevance of the activity.
- Awareness of increasing knowledge.
- Taking action and seeing a result occur because of what one has done.
- Using existing skills and acquiring new ones.
- Making observable progress, and being successful.
- Working with congenial people; being appreciated by them and contributing to a team effort.
- Experiencing a well-prepared and therefore status-conferring environment.

These benefits are not inherently difficult to provide, but they do not appear by magic. The game administrator has to be aware of player motivation as a serious issue and behave accordingly.

INTRODUCING THE GAME – PRACTICALITIES

Honesty is necessary between administrator and players. The administrator must think through his reasons for running a game and make a clear declaration to the players about what he hopes they will gain from playing it. In a sense, the game needs to be marketed. The next step is 'Make people do something themselves as soon as possible'. Here are some of the ways it can be achieved:

MINIMAL VERBAL BRIEFING

If the user has become familiar with the device, there is a great temptation to imagine that a verbal briefing will make things clearer than the written text. This can be an illusion. Games always start with a period of confusion when players do not know what to do and elaborate verbal briefing usually delays the start of this period without reducing its length. 'What to do' never really becomes clear until one tries to do it, and a much better strategy is to start the period of confusion early and be constantly available to answer questions. The great benefit of this policy is that when people ask questions they will be doing so because they want to know the answer. Similarly, when they study the players' instructions they will be doing so because they want to find specific information. Administrator briefings are basically attempts to guess beforehand what players *might* want to know and are less effective than waiting to divulge what they *do* want to know *when they want to know it.*

AGGRESSION

Press the playing teams to produce an early decision, despite all the complaints about inadequate time. Work expands to fill the time available for it and decisions made with two hours' debate will not be much better than decisions made after one hour's debate.

INVESTIGATION

The idea of a warm start can be put to good use by making players take over an existing company, and structuring that company so that it is in an unsatisfactory position. Players can then be required (as an initial task) to make some analysis of the inherited state and perhaps answer questions about it (e.g. 'What was their unit cost?'). This has two beneficial effects. In working out why previous decisions were *bad*, the players pick up some clues as to what decisions might be *good*. And it gives them a limited, finite task on which to get started when the broad task of 'Developing a new policy' might be hard to get into.

POSSIBLE INTERVENTIONS DURING PLAY

If circumstances demand totally fair competition throughout the event, the administrator is barred from intervening. Normally this is not the case and helpful interventions can take many forms.

INTERVENTION TO AVOID MISUNDERSTANDING

The imaginary nature of a game or simulation always leaves scope for genuine misunderstanding about what the rules mean, where the game boundaries lie, and how the various figures are made up. The administrator should ensure that doubts in these areas are quickly set right.

INTERVENTIONS TO ASSIST LEARNING

Playing teams commonly adopt a short-term focus, spending time on firefighting actions to correct bad results but not completing the basic groundwork that is necessary to conduct a business. The user who becomes familiar with any one game will be able to make a list of familiar errors, watch for them, and use them constructively. For instance, it is common for playing teams to:

- Fail to interpret the data on computer print-outs returned to them, and make decisions by guesswork despite the existence of factual data.

- Fail to make any long-term forecast which would allow them to work out a balanced production and marketing strategy.
- Fail to analyse their total costs into direct and indirect costs, and to make any sort of breakeven calculation.
- Fail to make any cost/benefit calculation matching a projected expense to the gain it is expected to win.

When these failures are apparent, the administrator should halt the progress of the game and make sure that everybody learns the necessary lessons and can benefit from them in play.

INTERVENING TO PROMOTE SUCCESS

Intervening to promote success is a controversial area, because in a competitive game it gives an unfair advantage. The administrators of one of the national business games would certainly not make helpful suggestions to any team, however badly it was playing. Other situations are less competitive, and the dangers of preferrential treatment must be balanced against the demotivating effect of continued failure. And some of the reasons for failure are very understandable. Assumptions might, for instance, be drawn from a real-world environment which do not apply in the present game; such as the tendency of people in the pharmaceutical industry to believe that one can build up a position in the market which will then be easy to defend – a characteristic not always replicated in games. Intervention to set a team right is frequently repaid by greatly improved motivation and a better chance of learning from the rest of the game. A useful lesson from this is that success, even if obtained with outside help, is a substantial motivator. Just the feeling 'We now know how to do it' makes a difference.

MANIPULATING THE MARKET AND THE ENVIRONMENT

The user interested in maximizing the learning value of a game should have no compunction about altering market sizes to make the task a bit easier (if the teams are struggling) or a bit harder (if they are not being sufficiently challenged). This behaviour is no different from that of the athletics coach, who puts players through training routines that test them and challenge them but avoids giving targets that are beyond their capabilities. The downturns ought always to be so scheduled that they are negotiated before the end of the game and the final experience is one of success.

EXAMINING PROCESS ISSUES

A team session which reviews the team's cooperative skill can be helpful if kept strictly separate from gaming sessions. This review should concentrate on what happened on an interpersonal level, perhaps using the terminology of a behaviour-typing instrument.

END-GAME REVIEWS

Reviews are discussed extensively in Chapter 10, but in respect of computer-controlled business games there is an argument for keeping the briefs to a limited time-scale. One reason is that further play is not possible and it is not very exciting to receive advice that one has no chance to put into practice. Also, the presence of several teams make plenary sessions – all teams reporting in turn – rather boring and repetitive. It may be better to highlight the learning points at appropriate moments during the play of the game and to keep the final review brief and cheerful. One way of handling it is to pose the question 'If you started again, knowing what you know now, how would you shape your policy?'

In respect of reviews, the academic world, and the quasi-academic world of open learning, have the opportunity to refer back to a game experience through project work. This seems an excellent way to conduct considered reflection outside the slightly anti-climactic atmosphere which exists when a game has just been won and lost.

COMPUTER-LINKED VARIATIONS

New variations in game use are constantly appearing, some of them directly generated by the capability of the microcomputer. These are departures, in some way, from the original repetitive cycle of decision and result.

PREPARED FUTURES

Players can be asked to take over an imaginary company and run it in a non-interactive way through a time period that has been pre-programmed for them. This can contain 'normal' events like a modest downturn in the economy or crises like an inability to obtain supplies. These are usually direct-access games and any number of alternative futures can be provided. Each cycle ends with a set of accounts and an update about the environment.

RE-PLAYS

Rather than move onwards through time, players can be allowed to tackle the same problem several times to work out the optimum policy by analysis and repetitive trial. Alternatively, they can move onwards but have the state of affairs after each trial recorded. It is then possible to go back to any chosen point and say 'Let's start again from there.' The recording of decisions and results also allows subsequent analysis of what was done, or even prompts and warnings from the program when potentially dangerous decisions are made. The technology enables the player situation to become quite similar to the real-life situation of a director as far as intellectual analysis and decision-making is concerned.

RESEARCH

The capability of the microcomputer to provide information can be used to structure a game that is research-dependent, the need for information having to be recognized, and relevant information sought out.

For example, operational details that might not always be known at board level can be hidden. For instance, the main result screen might show a downturn in annual sales with no clear reason. Amongst the options available to players would be the opportunity to view production department records and these, when called up, might show a mid-year problem which resulted in the company being out of stock for several weeks and therefore losing sales. Production could have increased towards the year end so that the main result screen showed stock in hand and gave no indication that this problem had ever happened. This is the 'drill down' effect characteristic of executive information systems.

TIME CONTROLS

The time keeping capabilities of the microcomputer can be used to spring surprises on teams, or to enforce time limits – so that (for instance) a team that has *not* done something by a given time experiences a particular problem and a team that *did* take action is spared.

'WHAT IF' MODELS AS AIDS TO DECISION-MAKING

The idea of 'what if' models has been mentioned in connection with major business game competitions, but there is nothing complex about the technology and it can be invoked at any level. Such a model might, for instance, allow players to enter their own preferred strategy and assumed strategies for their opponents. One person might argue 'Let's suppose that they (an opposing team) did that. How would it affect us?' Somebody else might counter with 'They won't do that – look at the effect it would have on their own gross margin!' Thus the level of discussion becomes quite sophisticated and realistic.

VARIATIONS INTRODUCING QUALITATIVE ELEMENTS

The mechanistic nature of business games and their 'omission of critical strategic factors such as organizational culture, structure, politics and other "soft" human dimensions' (Ken Peattie) have long been recognized. However, the importance of their apparent objectivity and rationality caused any human interference with a workable game to appear rather like sacrilege. One used a game as it was meant to be used by the author, or not at all. The climate has now changed, and business games are seen as components that can be engineered into a learning situation and modified, if necessary, to introduce qualitative elements. Here are some ways to achieve this.

QUALITATIVE INPUTS THROUGH CASE STUDIES

One method is to create descriptive case studies with limited choice solutions. The solution chosen by a team is keyed in with the other decision variables and the computer is programmed to respond in a different way to each allowed answer. Almost any degree of sophistication is possible, such as a condition which says 'If they do that in time period 2, then unless they also do that in time period 4 then this is going to happen to them in time period 7.' Similarly, it is possible to use a case study answer to unlock new events, causing a situation to be presented to one team that is not presented to another. The case studies can even be written in such a way that the answers are a choice between spoken words. In that way an inconsiderate answer can lead, say, to an important employee starting the search for a better job and leaving three time periods later.

EXTERNALLY JUDGED ADDITIONS

Traditionally, a high degree of objectivity was seen as a strength in business games. Those that were believed to be well-researched and accurate were seen to offer players something better than the subjective impressions of a teacher. At the very least they provided a constant evaluation and the model discriminated reliably in favour of those with the analytical skill to grasp how it worked. This is a reasonable viewpoint, but it does not entail the rigid exclusion of anything that is subjective. If that mental shift is made, the door is open for more subjective additions than case study choices with predetermined responses, for example an unashamed input of 'non-computer scores' that are converted into cash benefits or penalties and added to the existing financial results. For instance, role-playing staff members may descend upon the teams and reveal themselves as potential customers, overseas trading partners, or VAT inspectors – anything that gives them a legitimate reason for testing the knowledge of the team or its effectiveness as a group. After interacting with the team, they give a score for how well the team handled the visit and it is entered to the computer program.

PERSONALITY FOR THE COMPUTER

Another idea is to make the model respond to inputs with a degree of bias. In the game Negotiate with the Japanese the program prepared by TJA Enterprises causes the machine to assess the negotiating proposals entered by the teams not by a traditional, western calculation of implied short-term gain but against Japanese concepts of how a desirable trading partner ought to behave.

VARIATIONS THAT REPOSITION THE GAME ITSELF

Distinct from the previous variations are those which do not so much modify the game but position it within a learning strategy. This is perhaps the most interesting type of development, since it no longer accepts the game itself as the principal focus, but looks at larger issues to decide whether, and how, a game relates to them.

CREATING INDUSTRIAL GROUPS

Playing teams can be regarded as member companies within an industrial group, one representing the parent company and others representing subsidiaries. This superimposes on the 'objective' fact of a subsidiary firm's profitability the subjective fact of group strategic objectives. It makes it possible, say, for a commercially successful subsidiary to be sold off against its will because its activities do not fit within 'The overall strategic plan'. An interesting example is described by D.F. Cain in a paper from 'The User's Conference' of the April Training Executive, November 1991. This relates to an activity at Newcastle Business School, using EXECUTIVE 3000, and includes the comment about a controversial take-over:

> 'Each group believed that the other was guilty of withholding information and remained sceptical about the possibility of achieving fruitful cooperation. Formal communication therefore proved difficult. Informally, even humorous asides were likely to be attributed with an edge their authors had not intended.'

CHANGING STAFF

Another option is to change over personnel of teams. Everybody can be gathered at a central location and told:

> 'Some time in your lives you are likely to be transferred without notice. This is going to be simulated now. Some of you are not going back to the room you came from but are going to a new post in a new team in a new location.'

This gives the people transferred the experience of entering a new environment and adapting to it. It gives the rest of the team the experience of integrating a new member.

INTER-TEAM NEGOTIATIONS

Another way to introduce the human element is to build a model in which teams can negotiate with each other to improve the environment in which they are trading. An example might be to allow a cost reduction in some purchase provided they both buy from the same supplier but that cost reduction is offered only if joint purchases reach a certain volume. Each team might then try to persuade the other to take more than it requires in order to reach the benchmark at which unit price would fall.

The descriptions and suggestions of this chapter may encourage game users to take an imaginative and proactive approach. There are many ways of enhancing the value of a game; some of them demand technical knowledge, but others are a matter of administrative detail within the competence of the development specialist.

9 Games and teambuilding

Management games can contribute to teambuilding in two ways. They can be used to make organizational systems work better, and they can improve the utilization of the skills and abilities of employees.

BUREAUCRACY AND TEAMWORK

There is a degree of conflict between bureaucratic organization and teamwork. The conflict is not meant to exist, and there are many leaders of bureaucratic organizations who say with pride 'I have a very good team'. 'Surely', the argument goes, 'if every member knows what he is supposed to do, and has the skill to do it, and does it conscientiously; and if all the functions are integrated smoothly, then that constitutes a perfect team?' By one definition it does, but changing times have caused us to question the validity of that definition.

BUREAUCRACY IS BECOMING INADEQUATE

Traditional bureaucratic organization has revealed some in-built weaknesses when exposed to the modern environment. Businesses now face fierce international competition, and in the public sector we want more and better services – of a more and more costly type – without being too keen on paying for them. There is great pressure for efficiency, and sometimes this has resulted in a changed method of operation that appears to be an improvement on what went before. In a process that looks rather like natural selection, the emergence of a variant strain has made us question whether existing practices are the best possible. Methods that used to be alright are no longer alright.

BUREAUCRACY LIMITS THOUGHT

A common weakness of bureaucratic organization is that in assigning responsibility for certain tasks to specific people, it permits functionally-bounded thinking. It becomes possible for an office-holder to concentrate exclusively on the responsibilities with which he *has* been charged and to regard all other responsibilities as 'nothing to do with me'. The least harmful consequence of this attitude is that one functional manager comes across an item of information that might be useful to another and simply does not notice it. The most harmful consequence is deliberate (but unprovable) sabotage to prevent the other from gaining ground.

BUREAUCRACY IS APT TO FAVOUR INTERNAL COMPETITION

The idea of gaining ground is linked to the fact that a bureaucracy is almost always a power structure as well. Office-holders within it want to progress upwards, and this generally requires the approval of superiors. Pleasing a superior can become more important to an individual than campaigning for the things he believes to be right. This is not certain to happen – there are bureaucracies where the goodwill of office-holders makes them work very well – but the weaknesses of the system invite such behaviour.

BUREAUCRACY EMPLOYS ONLY PART OF A PERSON

The idea of defining the job to be done, and the skills and qualifications needed, implies that what the hiring organization wants is knowledge, skills and abilities rather than the human being in which these attributes reside. It sounds ridiculous, put like that, but provided he executes competently the work for which he was employed, many organizations are not interested in the rest of the person. For decades this was not a problem: it was accepted as a normal part of the employment contract. However, there has been a subtle change in the way people view the relationship between work and the rest of life, and it can now be argued that:

1. Those benefits that are assumed to be conferred have been down-graded through the disappearance of the 'job for life' concept – a benefit few employers can offer.
2. Those benefits have been further down-graded by the fact that some of them are partially obtainable elsewhere. We have a society in which unemployment is uncomfortable, but not a threat to existence.

The benefits of employment are always balanced, mentally, against what one has to give, and if one is receiving less benefit, then the 'trading balance', as one might call it, is disturbed. To restore the balance, the employer must give more or the employee must give less. Two ways in which the employer can give more are to *reduce* the negative aspects of work and to *increase* the positive aspects. One of the more negative factors which might be removed is the apparent need to leave much of one's personality at home. One of the positive aspects to be increased might be the opportunity to find at work an outlet for skills and abilities beyond those for which one was explicitly hired. In plain language, work could be made more enjoyable.

A NEW IDEAL

The negative aspects of traditional bureaucracy might not attract attention on their own. If there were no positive new ideas they might be accepted without question. However, new ideas do exist, as found in the following areas:

- From motivation theory
  A greater awareness of the psychological rewards obtainable from using and developing one's skills and cooperating voluntarily and effectively with others. The identification of these rewards with those found in other aspects of people's lives, which in a non-work environment would be described as 'I enjoy doing this. It's fun!'
- From psychology and behavioural science
  Knowledge of how personality can be matched with preferred roles/functions, so that in an integrated team people can perform the tasks they enjoy most. The idea that the team itself can become a source of psychological rewards – independently of the goal for which the team is striving.
- From sport and leisure
  Clear, high-profile evidence of the way top class teams develop a mutual understanding between members which takes them beyond the standards achievable by careful planning alone. Evidence of the intense effort people apply in pursuit of leisure activities, often enduring discomfort and hardship, which suggests that there is some unseen benefit outweighing all these (i.e. a proof that hard work can be enjoyable).

A VISION NOT YET REALIZED

When these ideas are brought together, a vision emerges of a work team in which each member has the following deep convictions:

- Personal well-being is linked to the well-being of the organization.
- Each member is valued as an individual human being and is encouraged to grow.
- All parts of the organization fulfil a necessary function and are linked together to achieve a worthwhile goal.
- Each member is entitled to be interested in all aspects of the operation. This is not cancelled out by the fact that he has special responsibilities in a limited area.
- Each member has a duty to examine every suggestion for improvement in his area of responsibility, whatever the source.
- Each member should act as one who wants the organization to succeed, and as one who knows that his efforts in that regard will be appreciated.
- Each member is concerned about other members.

HURDLES TO OVERCOME

The creation of this team attitude is a long haul. It is a matter of faith, and faith depends on evidence. At present few organizations inspire the convictions listed above and some inspire the opposite. There are not enough models to follow.

To illustrate the difference between what is and what might be, imagine a manager on holiday in another country and meeting, socially, local people who work for a company like his own, but work, say, in production while he works in sales. This notional sales manager, if he holds a traditional bureaucratic view, might know nothing beyond the confines of his own function and be utterly uninterested in the learning potential of the encounter. If, instead, he is a committed member of a 'real' company team then he would have a reasonable knowledge of the overall working of his firm. He would be able to recognize useful information and pass it on to his own production people. The thrust of current ideas about teamwork is that people should become able and willing to cooperate intelligently across bureaucratic boundaries.

At present there are two difficulties involved in this approach. Firstly, people do not know enough about the overall working of the system in which they play a specialized role: they cannot identify opportunities for cooperation because they are not sufficiently aware of what 'the other person' is doing. Secondly, people's relationships with other system members are not of a kind that enables them to communicate fully and freely. Development practitioners seek to address both these problems, and management games are one of the methods they use.

HELPING SYSTEM MEMBERS TO KNOW THEIR SYSTEM

USING KNOWLEDGE-BASED BUSINESS GAMES

For this purpose, the decision-making games that ask the student to run an imaginary enterprise are often used. They usually feature the relationship between different functions, making clear how these interact by allowing, say, a mismatch between production and sales which leads to an avoidable cost. Thus if production exceeds sales demand, there is a cost of storing the excess goods until they can be sold. If sales demand exceeds the quantity produced, then the costs incurred in generating the demand (salespeople, perhaps, and advertising) are wasted. In a game about the public service the variables would be different, showing, perhaps, how constraints at different stages between the time of the admission and the time of discharge of a hospital patient affect the total numbers treated. In both cases players with experience of a single department can gain a deeper understanding of the total system.

The repetitive format of computer-controlled business games is specially suitable for these objectives because mistakes are not catastrophic and can be allowed to happen, which highlights both their importance and the ease with which they can arise. In all but the simplest games some of the following mismatches are likely:

- Poor coordination of production and marketing policies.
- Heavy selling of low-margin products because nobody listened to the accountant.
- Poor quality production because nobody listened to the personnel specialist when he advised spending money on training.
- A heavy interest burden because nobody thought to work out the probable cash flow and make optimal arrangements with the bank.
- Erratic dividend policy because no provision was made for depreciation and unforeseen plant replacement swallowed up all the money.

As integrative tools, enabling players to comprehend 'how the whole thing fits together', business games are particularly strong.

ASSIGNING IN-GAME ROLES

The chance of significant errors (with the learning opportunites they bring) can be increased by setting up the game so that individual players have specific roles. However, this may have to be more formal than just assigning titles, for in a competitive situation a team may be so concerned to do well that they cross boundaries anyway. It may be helpful to emphasize the point by dividing the written instructions so that each functional manager has only his own data, or even by separating different role-players geographically.

SCOPE OF THE GAME

When using a game to study the system within which people are operating, the question of boundaries arises. Every system is itself part of a larger system and there is little point in examining the area one already knows. Functional managers are likely to benefit from a game about general management problems: managers of a wholly-owned subsidiary will benefit from studying the environment of a publicly quoted company: managers of a national firm will benefit from studying multi-national operations. It is important that the playing of such a game should be supported by genuine expertise in operating the larger system, for the lessons to be learnt from it may need interpretation.

HELPING SYSTEM MEMBERS TO VALUE COMMUNICATION

The influence of past habits is so strong that people may accept the need for broad knowledge of their own system, and yet not appreciate the full value of open communication. After all, a traditional bureaucracy has a workable procedure for inter-departmental communication – 'Identify the department which specializes in the subject about which you want to know, and ask them.' This approach worked well enough when the problems confronted were familiar and limited, in an organization set up for a specific purpose within a near-static environment. People could formulate their questions clearly and locate the probable source of the answer. The current environment brings new problems, and the basis of an enquiry may well be 'Here is my problem as I see it. Do you have any ideas that might help me?' This is not a case of somebody providing an answer 'from stock'. The two parties have to consider the problem cooperatively and in depth, neither of them knowing for sure that an answer even exists. The situation can be illustrated by an adaptation of the Johari Window as shown in Figure 9.1. Imagine the large square as the end view of a tank filled with rather murky water. It represents the total expertise of two people and is viewed from different points by the questioner (me) and the person I am asking for help (the respondent – you). Each of us can see items that are close to us, but the bottom of the tank is obscure to me and the far side is obscure to you. To show this, the square is divided The situation in each of those squares is as follows:

1. Top left
   Things **known to me** and **known to you**. This is the old area of cooperation. An area in which we each know what the other possesses.
2. Bottom left
   Things **unknown to me** but **known to you**. This is an area of expertise that you possess and which is therefore part of our joint total stock. But I do not know that you have it, and therefore I do not ask you questions about it. I miss out on a valuable source of information.
3. Top right
   Things **known to me** but **unknown to you**. This is an area of expertise that I know myself but which you do not realize I possess. In trying to help with my

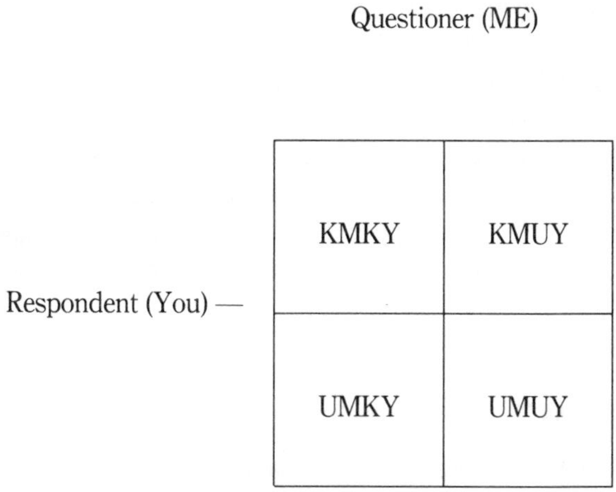

Questioner (ME)

Respondent (You) —

KMKY	KMUY
UMKY	UMUY

Figure 9.1 Identifying our joint stock of knowledge and expertise

problem you might discount certain options (and not mention them) because so far as you knew our joint stock of expertise did not include these items.

4. Bottom right

   Things **unknown to me** and **unknown to you**. This is the area of which neither of us is aware, because we have never examined it from the position of the current common problem. Once we do so, we may find ourselves saying 'Well, if you can really do *that* then I feel sure I can carry it on and do *this*!'

The suggestion is that the more we know about each other's skills, abilities and characteristics, the more competent we will be at finding solutions to problems. So knowing about our colleagues becomes an end in itself. We are not doing it just to solve one particular problem, but because of the extra general capability it gives us.

Some of the management games now in use seek to illustrate this argument. The exercise Sister-Teams referred to earlier, features cooperative opportunites which teams can only exploit if they communicate at a level deep enough to reveal that they have a common interest and a differing mix of resources. The argument is that many cooperative opportunities are missed in real life and that this does not worry us because we simply press on without ever knowing that they were there.

FULL AND FREE COMMUNICATION

Even when human beings are aware that effective communication might bring benefits, they do not always attempt it. The principal reason is perhaps that it might also bring pain. Each of us, in revealing what we think and feel about a subject or a person expose ourself to the possibility of opposition, scorn, ridicule or antagonistic action. So far as an answer to this problem exists, it seems to be that knowledge helps: self-knowledge, and knowledge about the other party. It then becomes possible to handle the relationship with more confidence: to identify the areas in which trust and cooperation are possible, and to steer clear of those where interests conflict. It also enables one to avoid the many conflicts that are quite unnecessary – those that spring up because one person makes erroneous assumptions about another because he fails to interpret that other person's behaviour. This belief that knowledge helps underlies many of the activities undertaken by development specialists. They are in essence no more than attempts to encourage people within organizations to know more about each other – not as office-holders, but as human beings. What are the methods employed?

DIAGNOSTIC INSTRUMENTS

There are several questionnaires that purport to tell us about ourselves: to analyse our personality and fit us into categories. These are useful, because facts are known about these categories and we can learn how people of our category typically interact with others. We can also discover where the people we work with fit in, and what attitudes people in their categories typically have. These instruments explain behaviour. They allow us to understand it, and if one understands something it is much easier to relate to. One knows what one can safely do, and what one cannot do, and it becomes possible to plan. Instead, perhaps, of regarding the other party as a completely unpredictable volcano, likely to explode without warning at any moment, we can see him as reasonable enough provided we can control our own behaviour. These instruments have varying degrees of academic acceptability and complexity. One that is easy to use, and gives valuable insights quickly, is the strength deployment inventory of Dr Elias Porter, already referred to in an earlier dicussion (see p.19).

FAMILIARIZATION EXERCISES

Icebreakers make a start on the process of 'becoming acquainted'. A more elaborate exercise commonly used takes two different occupational groups and requires each side to work through three questions. The first is 'What do we think about them?' The second is 'What do we think about ourselves?' The third is 'What do we think that they think about us?' When the work is complete, the parties share their perceptions.

Another approach is to use value-loaded exercises. A range of controversial subjects is posted, and triads created of one observer plus people with two opposing views. The task of each person in turn is to discover what the other believes, and why, without obtruding their own views or creating an argument. The observer is present to ensure that only constructive questioning is used, and the reflection of views in the manner of 'Am I correct in saying that your reasons for so-and-so are XYZ?' An alternative is to use a ranking exercise in which the rankings that come naturally to people's minds will reflect their personal values. Perhaps the most obvious of these is that in which some imaginary disaster forces a choice about who should be saved and who should be left to die.

WORKING TOGETHER

The most frequently used technique to encourage teamwork is simply to ask people to undertake a joint activity and work together in pursuit of an objective. This method seems to produce much more dramatic results than talking sessions or the academic exploration of personality. This is perhaps due to a greater time allocation, or perhaps to the fact there is physical action of some sort involved – and the evidence of deeds as well as the evidence of words. Perhaps it is because there is an objective, at which one succeeds or fails and which provides a meaningful challenge. Whatever the reasons, almost any concerted cooperative activity will have some sort of teambuilding benefit, and there is great variety in the devices used. However, one can make better choices amongst activities after asking a few more questions. Assuming that working together increases mutual knowledge and understanding, are there some areas of knowledge that offer more benefit than others, and are there conditions under which an activity will be more or less effective?

SHARED ACTIVITIES – WORK-RELATED OR NOT?

The general objective of the activity is to deepen cooperation between team members by enhancing communication and mutual understanding. This usually happens through increased mutual respect, each person gaining a higher regard for the other and therefore being more inclined to make the effort and take the psychological risks that serious communication demands. This change has to be based on receiving new information about each other and therefore work-related activities tend not to be chosen: the aspects of themselves people reveal at work are already well-known to their colleagues. If they are going to learn more about each other, they need to see each other in different circumstances.

If this is true, why are conventional computer-controlled business games so often used for teambuilding purposes? They are distinctly work-related, yet players commonly identify their greatest gain from such an experience as increased ability to cooperate effectively with their colleagues. A possible answer is that while the subject matter is familiar, the manner in which game teams cooperate is quite different from what happens in real life. As a game team they are physically together, and all have a voice in all decisions. The real-life situation places them in different offices, not meeting together very often (and then in a formal situation) and having to accept that many decisions will be made unilaterally within the appropriate department. The degree of interaction within the 'team' of a conventional bureaucracy is much more limited than the interaction between a team physically together and dedicated to an immediate common task. Business game players frequently gain the following benefits:

- An in-depth knowledge of people from a different part of the company with different views and different values.
- Learning about the inadequacy of individual knowledge, in the sense that almost any 'expert' answer can be improved by the input of competent and dedicated colleagues.

Therefore the use of business games for teambuilding does not invalidate the argument that teambuilding activities generally are intended to reveal *new* information. The new knowledge likely to be gained may include the following:

- New awareness of skills and abilities possessed by colleagues.
- New awareness of common interests.
- New awareness of the value attached to the roles that colleagues play in the team, and the qualities of character that enable them to do so.

The last of these ideas needs some explanation and is linked to the idea of content and process in group work, which was discussed earlier. The qualities that enable a person to contribute to effective group process are largely qualities of character. They are quite distinct from qualities of intellect, but we tend to know very little about them. At work, people are associated with each other because of the particular posts that they fill and their dealings with each other are naturally centred around the duties of those posts. A person working with a plumber comes to know quite quickly whether he is a good plumber or a poor plumber, and a person associated with an accountant knows whether the accounting is well done. But the skills for which a person is hired are a small part of the person as a human being, and vast areas of personality never come to light. It is a common state to know the plumber or the accountant but not to know the human being.

In an effective group, however, there is a need for what may be called social skills as well as strictly technical skills. A person has value to the team if he is seen to display certain characteristics, for example:

- You can always talk to and receive a sympathetic hearing.
- The one who is keen and will always force the team to start on the job.
- The one who looks ahead, sees the problems, and prepares the team for them.
- The one who is naturally creative and can think of novel solutions.
- The one who helps colleagues who do not understand.
- The one who searches out people, ideas and materials that will help the team.
- The one who helps the team to coordinate its ideas.
- The one who won't give up.
- The one who won't accept poor solutions.
- The one who provides the team with a few laughs when conditions are tough.
- The one who double-checks solutions to make sure that the team has not made any stupid errors.

These are qualities of *character* which relate to 'the sort of person one is'. Management games can create a situation in which these process-related qualities assume great importance and bestow status on members who might not acquire it through their knowledge-related skills. Games of this type are, so to speak, making process issues their own subject matter. It is worth noting that one of the best-known categorizations of personal qualities – that of Dr Meredith Belbin, was developed in the context of teams playing a business game.

COACHING

When people are working together, the skilled external observer can sometimes see patterns in the activity, and opportunities for improvement, which are not otherwise noticed. This idea of observation and analysis has drawn new strength from the high profile of top-level competitive sport and the emergence of the sports coach as an influential figure. One of the many contributions of a coach is to watch his team in action, analyse its performance, and discuss it with the players afterwards. An important difference between sport and industry is that the latter has no equivalent to the bounded time-scale of 'a match' – the activity is continuous, taking place in many locations at the same time and is not observable as a totality. The coach cannot, for instance, be at a meeting of the Finance Department, *and* at a meeting of the Marketing Strategy Group, but if all the team members are engaged at the same time in a management game, then observation of their cooperative skill is possible. The situation is not identical to their everyday work, but it is close enough to raise valuable questions. The coach can point to cases of misunderstanding, to options not explored and to opportunities missed, and ask 'If it can happen in here, might it not happen also out there? Are there real-life parallels which, if identified and worked on, might improve your level of success?'

SHARED ACTIVITIES – SUBJECT MATTER

Choosing suitable activities can be made easier by observing two principles:

1. Ensure that the activity is enjoyable; and,
2. Give everybody a chance to shine.

A point to re-emphasize is that motivation comes from many different sources, and for some people team membership may be a powerful, even a dominating motivator. These people are not particularly concerned with what the team is trying to achieve, they just like being a part of it. For this force to operate, for the team itself to become a source of motivating rewards (as opposed to the conventional extrinsic rewards) the teamworking experience has to be an enjoyable one. A supposed teambuilding experience that brings no enjoyment will actually be a team destruction experience.

This idea has powerful implications for matching people to the activity and for setting tasks with an appropriate level of difficulty. The problems are most clearly seen in outdoor management development (OMD) where huge gains are achievable by somebody who succeeds where he previously believed himself incompetent. If, instead, he fails yet again and confirms his poor self-image then the activity has been counterproductive. Sometimes the groups sent on OMD activities include a few who positively hate them, and spend a miserable time dragging round after their colleagues.

The best outcome of a teambuilding activity is that everybody should learn something positive and good about everybody else, which means giving all of them some chance to display their good qualities. If the administrator of such an exercise knows the participants well then activities can be almost tailor-made, but the next best option is to have a multifaceted activity, to make every part of it different, and to allow no single part of it to continue for too long. A common form is to separate participants into teams and give each a list of points-earning tasks. They must review the skills, interests and abilities that their team possesses, choose which tasks to do, allocate them to suitable people or groups, monitor progress, and decide when success has been reached or when a task should be abandoned. The format is flexible, allowing the integration of different types and lengths of task. For instance, a paper-and-pencil ranking exercise might be followed by a clay pigeon shoot, and that followed by a logic puzzle and a motorized search. It should certainly include activities which require the following skills:

- Manual dexterity.
- Patience and determination.
- Skill with numbers.
- Skill with words.
- Imagination and creativity.
- Accuracy and precision.
- Ability to work with others.
- Ability to work alone.
- Physical strength.
- Mental agility.

Different structures can be imposed upon this format. For example, each team can have an appointed leader and the 'management group' so constituted can negotiate task allocation with the administrator. The leader is thus in the position of having to know his people, and try to obtain the sort of tasks that they will find motivating. Another variation is the use of the joker concept, by which a team identifies the task it feels best qualified to perform well, and claims double points for it. A third variation is to judge a subjective task on the Eurovision Song Contest model – a team gives a rating for each of its competitors' performances, but not for its own.

The administration of these events needs to be smooth and professional, especially in regard to quick scoring and the display of results.

10 Debriefs, reviews and alternatives

The debriefing process is important to game users: one naturally wants to maximize the value of an event. Yet there is a danger of becoming mentally trapped by the terminology and thinking that that there *must* be a review/debrief or that the method is constant and invariable. There are times when it proves to be the most valuable part of the whole event, and there are times when it damages the outcome by denying participants the chance to puzzle out meaning for themselves.

It is also possible to become fixated upon the idea that a review/debrief comes *after* an activity, when it may be more useful at some intermediate point. The true objective is not to conform to some purist notion of 'the right way to do it' but to maximize the value of the session. A dramatic illustration of this can be found in the game sessions that are run for purely motivational reasons so that a team experiences the bonding effect of an enjoyable day. Such a day might concentrate on activities that are known to give pleasure and deliberately avoid all reference to the authority-dominated world of work. The person running such a day might be told '*Don't* contaminate the day with reviews and debriefs! They will damage the atmosphere of freedom and fun that we want to create!'

This example reveals the difficulty of defining 'learning', for while the word itself is avoided, the intention of such teambuilding activities *is* learning – related in the sense that it aims at attitude-change. Those who organize such days hope that participants will learn something about the team – the work team – as a source of rewards. The subtly-presented message is 'Interacting with these people can be enjoyable'. In fact, the use or avoidance of debriefing depends upon the type of learning that is being encouraged. That in turn depends on beliefs about the learning process and upon the subject matter. A debriefing session can take at least five different forms:

1. Informal comment of an anecdotal type around the bar. This may have no apparent learning value but may be very good for intra-team relationships.
2. Small groups of learners forming spontaneously to offer each other feedback, and possibly leading to learning contracts between the members.
3. A tutor-monitored session which relies heavily on the feedback of appointed observers.

4. A tutor-led session in which the personal views of participants are elicited by open-ended questions.
5. A tutor-led session in which predetermined lines of questioning are used to elicit the 'right' answers.

In some of these sessions the tutor or facilitator has no control over what is happening and some might contend that they do not constitute a review or debrief at all.

DIFFERENT PERSPECTIVES ON THE LEARNING PROCESS

Several answers are possible to the question 'What drives the learning process?' Is it forces external to the learner which say 'This is what you need to learn, and this is how to learn it?' Or is it the personal motivation of the skilled learner who can identify his own needs and meet them in his own way? A game user tending to the former view may favour formal reviews and debriefs since they allow 'reinforcement of the principal learning points' and reimposition of the control that was relaxed when it was decided to use a game or simulation. A user tending to the latter concept will see reviews as something to be left to the learners themselves, or even abandoned. The argument runs thus 'If a formal game review is needed, that just proves that I have failed to create in the participants a proper understanding of the active learning process.'

Of course, both approaches to learning have strengths and weaknesses. The 'free' approach is strong on motivation and enjoyment but wholly dependent on the learning skills of participants. The 'controlled' approach can sometimes reduce the enjoyment of the activity and even introduce the counter-productive element of fear. Here is a case that could be handled in different ways:

> A game took place outdoors, requiring the planning of quite detailed 'moves' that had then to be carried out quickly and in order by different group members. The complexity meant that control had to be entrusted to some 'caller' who shouted out each move in turn, having written down the agreed sequence on papers attached to a clipboard. A strong wind blew several sheets on the clipboard out of order, the caller lost his place, and the team effort collapsed in chaos.

The similarity of this example to a work situation is obvious. The caller knew it was a windy day and could easily have avoided the error by forethought and attention to detail – qualities that are necessary in many types of work and have a similar effect on team results. Thus the game situation has potential for work-related learning. Is this learning achieved? This depends on the attitude of the person. The skilled learner may think 'What I did in that game is a little like what I did at work last Friday. Maybe there is a message for me. Maybe I need to organize myself a little better.' But not everybody has this reflective attitude. Many will not see the parallels and will need to have them suggested through a game review. The circumstances of that review may be threatening, leading to denial of the parallel and comments like 'I would naturally not do that in a serious situation.' Present practice tends towards maintaining a degree of control in reviews and debriefs, for reasons such as these:

- Despite defensive reactions, the lessons offered are usually taken to heart in the end.
- Reviews enable the administrator to demonstrate that the planned learning points have at least been 'covered' – even if that only means 'transmitted' rather than 'received'.
- Reviews help participants who prefer direct instruction to be clear about what they are supposed to have learnt.
- Without reviews there is a real chance that connections with the world of work will never be made: people will recollect and discuss details of the game but will not recognize the messages it offers.
- Sophisticated learning skills of the type that make a tutor-controlled review unnecessary are comparatively rare. Even amongst experienced, well-educated people there is still a tendency to compartmentalize life and to see the experiences of work and play as quite distinct. Most people are not actively looking for this sort of parallel.

The current emphasis on measuring training effectiveness favours the more controlled review methods. They are therefore sometimes seen as a *must* and their drawbacks overlooked. Amongst those drawbacks are the following considerations:

- They provide prior identification of 'what ought to be learned' and therefore reinforce a traditional attitude to the process and do little to promote what might be a better approach.
- They are susceptible to manipulation by the user, so that specific learning points are emphasized in the review whether or not the experience of the game substantiates them.
- They are sometimes seen as a way to ensure a favourable response to questionnaires asking 'Was it a good course?'
- They are sometimes handled in an unimaginative and lacklustre way because they are seen as mandatory.
- They can make the overall impact of the session more 'worklike' and so detract from the motivation produced by 'game-like' methods.

The attitude of the game user towards the learning process is important enough to justify some further reflections. One subject on which to reflect is what characteristics make something 'serious' (work) or 'fun' (leisure)? Are these characteristics associated with an activity itself, or does the distinction exist only in the mind of the individual? Is it somehow bad for people to say 'It's only a game' and good for them to say 'This is really serious?' Do people learn less if they take the former attitude?

Perhaps what matters most is how hard the learner tries, and previously there has been a subconscious assumption that 'work-relevance' equates with seriousness and leads to maximum effort. Is this true? It implies that the rewards offered by work are more desirable, more motivating, and will generate more effort than other types of reward? Do they? Or is the whole concept a hangover from the industrial revolution that we have never thought to question? Some of the most motivated learners today are found in sport, where intense, high-profile competition has fuelled a search for improvement. The effort that sports coaches, and sportspeople put into researching knowledge, into planning and preparation, and into the analysis of every performance, is far greater than what is customary in commerce and industry. When asked why they make these efforts (for only a tiny minority will reach Olympic level) their answers tend to mention improvement, self-development, the pursuit of excellence, and the joy of increased capability. What such people reveal is a response to internal and personal incentives. At work, by contrast, it is not the individual but the organization that makes the decisions:

- It chooses what people will be asked to learn.
- It defines the rewards that may follow successful learning.
- It judges whether those rewards shall be given.

The old idea effectively says 'You should learn what the organization wants you to learn, because if you do then the organization will (might) give you the rewards it thinks you ought to want.' This lies behind every statement about 'principal learning points'. Perhaps it conceals the fact that personal learning might be richer and deeper if an event invited inputs from the learners. Inputs, that is, about what they felt they wanted to learn and about the range of rewards that learning it might bring. Obviously personal goals and organizational goals do not always coincide, but the point being made is that at present – with our jargon about 'principal learning points' – we are not even allowing a dialogue. We are making a unilateral decision without consultation.

VARIATIONS OF SUBJECT MATTER

Different subjects have different implications for the type of review required. This is best discussed by looking at the extremes. One such extreme arises with the identification of a specific and constant item of skill/knowledge that all the people concerned need to have and which they do not presently hold. An example might be the legal procedures governing dismissal which, if a manager fails to know and observe, could lead to a tribunal appearance. A review following such a training session can be almost like an examination – a means of allowing students to demonstrate whether they have or do not have the knowledge/skill required. There is no confusion: no opportunity for anybody to say 'It has rather a different meaning for me.' There is a clear, common message.

At the other extreme lie those subjects where data is subjective and open to interpretation, and 'deniable' by anybody who does not want to face up to it. The classic area is interpersonal behaviour: people find it difficult to cope with suggestions of inadequacy and will deny an accusation of being say 'abrupt and dismissive' when they will agree quite cheerfully that they are unable to spell. After a session directed at this sort of objective the review must be discreet, encouraging self-examination and avoiding accusations.

Subject areas of this type are distinct for two other reasons:

1. They are usually tackled with exercises that are loosely controlled and allow a high degree of freedom to participants. So the user never knows quite what is going to happen. An attempt to pre-plan a review can prove useless because none of the hoped-for lessons are substantiated by the experience.
2. There may be no message that is common, in the sense that all the participants need to learn it. For instance, an exercise might be directed at 'improving cooperative skills' and offer quite different messages to two people. One might learn that he needs to be more assertive, while another learns that he needs to become a better listener. Both these people might learn more effectively if encouraged to recognize their own needs rather than if asked to accept the comments of a tutor.

DIFFERENT PRACTICES FOR DIFFERENT APPROACHES

There are many practical tips, or tactics, for maximizing the effectiveness of reviews. Here are some of them, with comments about the circumstances in which they are most applicable.

CREATING IN LEARNERS A SELF-DIRECTING CLIMATE

If a self-directing climate is created, tutor-controlled reviews become unnecessary. However, this idealistic state is not often achieved. The idea is that learners should be so committed to learning from an experience that they will examine what each other has achieved and swap perceptions of how this came about and the effect it had, perhaps through discussion in small cooperative groups. This may extend to medium-term commitments in which one person agrees, say, to attend meetings as the 'shadow' of another and review that meeting later. Mutual 'learning contracts' can be formed.

Whether this is possible depends on the climate in an organization and can be totally misunderstood if the necessary climate does not exist. In organizations still favouring the ideal of 'clear, direct instruction' the facilitator who expounds this view will be seen as 'having no credibility' and 'failing in his responsibilities'. The necessary attitude to learning is not one that can be created in a single session: it is closely connected to organizational culture.

NARRATING AND SUMMARIZING

In more complex games, it may happen that participants are separated, geographically or by the function they perform. They can then have detailed knowledge of their own part, but be ignorant of the overall course of the event. It can be helpful for the tutor, or an observer, to provide an overview.

KEEPING A DIARY

The learning process, and a post-event review, can gain in value by requiring participants to record at certain times what they planned to do, and why. The technique works particularly well with business games of the decision-making type. Looking back objectively on a decision can throw light on the quality of the process by which one made it.

ACTING THE EXPERT

Participants can be told 'You have now worked through the problems of the exercise, which perhaps started you off in a slightly unfair position. Knowing what you know now, write some brief instructions that would enable the next participants to get it right first time.' People like to assume the expert role, and the demand that they should articulate the 'right' way to tackle the problem reinforces their learning about what that 'right' way is.

IN-GAME TUTOR INTERVENTION

One of the problems of post-event reviews is that the game players cannot go back and try again. They may learn from the review, but they are unable to put that learning to the test. Intervening part-way through a game can have a dramatic effect upon learning (and upon motivation) because it can allow players to play more effectively and gain a better result. There are serious points at issue here, for some games work by almost forcing participants to make the 'wrong' choice and then examine the causes of failure so that they become known and avoidable. (Almost like the cautionary tales of children's story books.) If learning success is thought to depend on game failure then intervention is a mistake. Sometimes game users over-exploit this tactic and participants are placed in a total 'no win' situation. One needs to remember that success is a motivator and that using new learning to 'get right' what one previously 'got wrong' is a powerful reinforcement of the learning process.

USING OBSERVERS TO REPORT ON BEHAVIOUR

The feedback offered after a game by trained observers can be most illuminating. There are several ways to use them:

- In conjunction with one of the behaviour-typing disciplines: observers are asked to count the incidence of behaviour like 'proposing', 'supporting' and 'blocking', reporting after the event on who did what and the effect they believe it had.
- They can be given a free-ranging brief and asked to report, in their own words, what they felt to be happening within the group at an interpersonal level.
- They can be given a list of developments that are thought likely to happen during an event. They are asked to record whether these developments occur and, if not, what happened instead. This is a very useful technique when the material used is probabilistic – meaning that certain things *usually* happen (which is why the exercise was chosen) but are not certain to occur.

BEHAVIOUR OF STAFF AND OBSERVERS

The previous comments relate more to the mechanics of reviews than to the personal behaviour of tutor/facilitator and observers. Yet this may be a greater variable than any other, determining whether people will share their experiences, opinions and emotions openly with each other. Some hints about personal behaviour, and especially the giving of feedback, are offered below.

ALLOW THE PARTICIPANTS THEMSELVES TO GIVE MEANING TO THE EXPERIENCE

Avoid stating what the lessons were 'meant' to be; instead ask general questions, listen to the answers, and put supplementary questions based upon those answers. By clarifying and rephrasing what participants say, help them to formulate conclusions that are valid for them personally.

DISTINGUISH BETWEEN FACT OR PERCEPTION

All observers must be familiar with, and committed to, the distinction between fact and perception. Whatever comments they offer should be identifiable as perceptions, not assertions of absolute reality. A good technique is to start from *actions* (giving observed examples) and move from these into interpretation.

DISTINGUISH BETWEEN CONTENT AND PROCESS

Staff and participants must be aware that subject matter and personal interaction are separate. Everybody must be clear about which is being discussed, and why.

SET CLEAR AND ACHIEVABLE OBJECTIVES

Ask for just one example of something that went well from the viewpoint of the participants, and one that went badly. Everybody should be able to think of an example of each type and this will begin conversation. One can then move on to why it went well/badly, and what other developments might have happened instead.

ASK FOR PARALLELS TO BE DRAWN WITH THE WORK SITUATION

Parallels are always more convincing if stated by the participants rather than the tutor. Participants have only one encounter with the exercise on which to base their conclusion, while the tutor knows what it is supposed to show, even if it fails to do so. Encourage work-related anecdotes that help to show how lessons from the game would apply at work. An intermediate step towards this may be similarities with experiences in other games.

ACCEPT THE LEGITIMACY OF DIFFERING VIEWS ABOUT WHAT HAPPENED

During the rapid interaction of an exercise, people form different impressions of what happened, and why. Accept these as adding variety and richness to the picture. Do not strive for some 'official version' which will not be recognized by the participants.

FUTURE GAME DEVELOPMENTS

A number of trends presently influencing the field of management games seem likely to continue. Technological development will certainly not slow down, and one will be able to simulate more situations with greater realism and greater ease. Variety will not slow down either – one reason being the increasingly international context of management education and the exchange of concepts between societies. More arguable is the extent to which work will be seen as an activity that should be rewarding in itself, and enjoyable, and therefore something to which game-playing can reasonably be linked. This is not an acceptable idea in all cultures. The issue will surely be influenced by how far practitioners are able to use games intelligently and effectively, so that the enjoyment is present but the learning outcome indisputable. It is an exciting field in which to be.

Index of suppliers of games

AD International
7 Oxhey Road, Watford, Hertfordshire WD1 4QF, Tel. 0923 224737, Fax 0923 210648.

Almeda Software
Friern Lodge, The Avenue, Ampthill, Bedfordshire MK45 2NR, Tel. 0525 402561, Fax 0525 840584.

April Training Executive Ltd
Chestnut Farm, Tarvin Road, Frodsham, Cheshire WA6 6XN, Tel. 0928 35868, Fax 0928 35352.

The Registrar
Ashridge Management College, Berkhamsted, Hertfordshire HP4 1NS, Tel. 0442 843491, Fax 0442 842382.

Claude Bourles
Gersafe, Institute de Psychologie et Sciences Sociales Appliquées, Université Catholique de L'Ouest, B.P. 808–49008 Angers Cedex, France, Tel. 01033 41 81 65 00, Fax 01033 41 81 66 09.

Nigel Bryant Associates
The Old Rectory, Great Brickhill, Buckinghamshire MK17 9AG, Tel. 0525 261563.

Dr Tony Bushell
Harrison Macey Ltd, 217 Silver Road, Norwich NR3 4TL, Tel. 0603 250312.

Business Simulation International
3–60 Mark Avenue, Ottawa, Ontario K1L 6A7, Canada, Tel. 0101 613 741 7575.

Cambridge University Press
The Edinburgh Building, Cambridge CB2 2RU.

G. Chapman
168 Upland Road, London SE22 0DQ. Tel. 081 299 1967.

Connaught Training Ltd
Gower House, Croft Road, Aldershot, Hampshire GU11 3HR, Tel. 0252 331551, Fax 0252 344405.

John R. Cooper, DMS, MBIM
7 St George's Avenue, Rugby, Warwickshire CV22 5PN, Tel. 0788 813736.

Chris Cunningham
Department of Geography and Planning, University of New England, Armidale, NSW 2351, New South Wales, Australia, Tel. 01061 67 73 2864, Fax 01061 67 71 1787.

Daedal Training Ltd
309 High Street, Orpington, Kent BR6 0NN, Tel. 0689 873637, Fax 0689 874183.

Rod Dawson
25 Cavendish Drive, Waterlooville, Hampshire PO7 7PJ, Tel. 0705 263703.

Philip Day
Convergent Communications Ltd, 17 Alfred Place, London WC1E 7EB.

I.A.S. Debenham
9 Roland Way, London SW7 3RF, Tel. 071 373 0585, Fax 0883 717526.

Deloitte & Touche Management Consultants Denmark
Ryesgade 29, DK-8000 Arhus C, Denmark, Tel. 01045 86 12 30 22, Fax 01045 86 12 07 13.

Peter Dye Associates
The Old Vicarage, Chiddingly, East Sussex BN8 6HE, Tel. 0825 872703, Fax 0825 872704.

Earthscan Publications Ltd
120 Pentonville Road, London N1 9JN.

Edit 515 Ltd
24 Buckstone Grove, Edinburgh EH10 6PF, Tel. and Fax 031 445 1405.

Chris Elgood Associates Ltd
Abacus House, Cranbrook Road, Hawkhurst, Kent TN18 4AR, Tel. 0580 713159, Fax 0580 712588.

P. Fish, MA, AMITD
Outdoor Consultant, The Yorkshire Dales Field Centre, The Square House, Church Street, Giggleswick, North Yorkshire BD24 0BG, Tel. 0729 822965.

J. M. Freeman
School of Management, UMIST, PO Box 88, Manchester M60 1QD, Tel. 061 200 3430, Fax 061 228 7040.

Edward Gropper
Missenden Abbey Management Centre, Great Missenden, Buckinghamshire HP16 0BD, Tel. 02406 6811, Fax 02406 6737.

Hall Marketing
Studio 11, Colman's Wharf, 45 Morris Road, London E14 6PA, Tel. 071 537 2982.

Ken Harry
117 Hare Lane, Claygate, Esher, Surrey KT10 0QY, Tel. 0372 462811, Fax 081 547 7029.

J. D. Hender
Public Sector Consultant, 16 South Avenue, Thorpe St Andrew, Norwich NR7 0EZ, Tel. 0603 35548.

Cranfield School of Management
Cranfield, Bedford MK43 0AL, Tel. 0234 750856, Fax 0234 751636.

Institute for Training in Intercultural Management
Celebesstraat 96, 2585 TP The Hague, The Netherlands, Tel. 01031 70 35 05054, Fax 01031 70 35 52003.

Dr Jan H. G. Klabbers
Oostervelden 59, 6681 WR Bemmel, The Netherlands, Tel. 01031 08811 62455.

Kogan Page
120 Pentonville Road, London N1 9JN.

LMG International
11 Albion Street, Hyde Park, London W2 2AS, Tel. 071 706 1208, Fax 071 706 2417.

Professor D. Langford
Department of Civil Engineering, University of Strathclyde, Glasgow G4 0NG.

Professor K. G. Lumsden
Director, The Esmée Fairbairn Research Centre, Heriot-Watt University, Riccarton, Edinburgh EH14 4AS, Tel. 031 451 3090, Fax 031 451 3002.

Peter McHardy
Leicester Business School, Bosworth House, Leicester Polytechnic, PO Box 143, Leicester LE1 9BH, Tel. 0533 551551, Fax 0533 517548.

Management Games Ltd
Methwold House, Methwold, Thetford, Norfolk IP26 4PF, Tel. 0366 728215, Fax 0366 728604.

Management Learning Resources Ltd
PO Box 28, Camarthen, Dyfed SA31 1DT, Tel. 0267 87661, Fax 0267 87315.

Dr R Matthew
Department of Civil Engineering, University of Bradford, Bradford BD7 1DP, Tel. 0274 383852, Fax 0274 383888.

Professor Dennis Meadows
IPSSR-Hood House, University of New Hampshire, Durham, NH 03824–3577, USA, Tel. 0101 603 862 2186, Fax 0101 603 862 1488.

Mott MacDonald
Demeter House, Station Road, Cambridge CB1 2RS, Tel. 0223 460660, Fax 0223 461007.

Northgate Training
Scarborough House, 29 James Street West, Bath BA1 2BT, Tel. 0225 339733.

PA Consulting Group
123 Buckingham Palace Road, London SW1W 9SR, Tel. 071 730 9000, Fax 071 333 5104.

Don Porter Associates, Inc.
2185 South Dixie, Dayton, Ohio 45409, USA, Tel. 0101 513 294 7330, Fax 0101 513 294 5186.

Dr Peter Reason
School of Management, University of Bath, Bath BA2 7AY, Tel. 0225 826792, Fax 0225 826473.

Nick Rints
Management Training Services, 5 Orchard Grove, Flackwell Heath, High Wycombe, Buckinghamshire HP10 9PT, Tel. and Fax 0628 523186.

George Ritchie
School of Defence Management, Royal Military College of Science, Shrivenham, Swindon, Wiltshire SN6 8LA, Tel. 0793 785258, Fax 0793 783878,

Royal Institution of Chartered Surveyors
12 Great George Street, London SW1P 3AD.

RTITB Services (Peter Hughes)
Capitol House, Empire Way, Wembley, Middlesex HA9 0NG, Tel. 081 902 8880, Fax 081 903 4113.

RTITB Services (D. P. Norris)
Capital House, Empire Way, Wembley, Middlesex HA9 0NG, Tel. 081 902 8880, Fax 081 903 4113.

Danny Saunders
Enterprise Unit, University of Glamorgan, Pontypridd CF37 1DL.

Peter Saunders
School of Management, Imperial College, 53 Exhibition Road, London SW7 2PG.

Professor A. Scott
The Esmée Fairbairn Research Centre, Heriot-Watt University, Riccarton, Edinburgh EH14 4AS, Tel. 031 451 3090, Fax 031 451 3002.

D. Sculli
Department of Industrial and Manufacturing Systems Engineering, University of Hong Kong, Hong Kong.

T.A.C. Shafto (Tutor Software)
Grove Lane, Wishaw, Sutton Coldfield, West Midlands B76 9PH, Tel. and Fax 021 351 4127.

Software Training International Ltd
The Maltings, 55 Bath Street, Gravesend, Kent DA11 0DF, Tel. 0474 329932, Fax 0474 335053.

Professor John D. Sterman
MIT Sloan School of Management, 50 Memorial Drive, Cambridge, MA 02139, USA, Fax 0101 617 258 7579.

Strategic People
48 Station Road, Chertsey, Surrey KT16 8BE, Tel. 0932 563213, Fax 0932 567257.

TJA Enterprises Ltd
5 The Glade, Buxton, Derbyshire SK17 6SL, Tel. 0298 26682.

Elizabeth Teather
Department of Georgraphy and Planning, University of New England, Armidale, NSW 2351, New South Wales, Australia, Tel. 01061 067 73 2864, Fax 01061 067 71 1787.

Bob Thompson
138 Bridgetown Road, Stratford upon Avon CV37 7JA, Tel. 0789 293267.

Total Business Services
29 Hollow Way Lane, Amersham, Buckinghamshire HP6 6DJ, Tel. 0494 721702.

Training House Inc.
PO Box 3090, Princeton, NJ 08543-3090, USA Tel. 0101 609 452 1505, Fax 0101 609 243 9368.

Understanding (Systems) Ltd
28 Orchard Avenue, Finchley, London N3 3NL, Tel. 081 346 4252, Fax 081 349 0417.

University of East Anglia (David A. Ward, Administrator BIMG)
Norwich NR4 7TJ, Tel. 0603 58220, Fax 0603 250619.

Verax Ltd
60 High Street, Odiham, Hampshire RG25 1LN, Tel. 0256 703355, Fax 0256 703086.

Wessex Training Services Ltd
5 Acorn Business Centre, Tower Park, Poole, Dorset BH12 4NZ, Tel. 0202 716088, Fax 0202 743163.

Hal Wilson
28 Parkside, Cambridge CB1 1JE, Tel. 0223 328736.

Winkler Marketing Ltd
Winkler Marketing House, 6 St George's Place, Brighton BN1 4GA, Tel. 0273 570144, Fax 0273 570133.

Douglas Wood
Manchester Business School, Booth Street West, Manchester M15 6PB, Tel. 061 275 6416, Fax 061 273 7732.

Gordon Wylie, Coopers & Lybrand Deloitte
PO Box 198, Hillgate House, 26 Old Bailey, London EC4M 7PL, Tel. 071 454 8576, Fax 071 236 2367.

Index